Joe's Story

The Remarkable Childhood Of Joe Sawley

Joyce Sawley

with Richard Patterson

HB

Honeybee Books

Published by Honeybee Books
Broadoak, Dorset
www.honeybeebooks.co.uk

Printed in the UK using paper from sustainable sources.

ISBN: 978-1-910616-11-6

FOREWORD

Having heard me recounting many a tale of my youth throughout our married life, I thought Joyce would have been sick of hearing them. I couldn't have been more wrong.

About 15 years ago, at the end of an evening during which I had shared with our guests a few stories from my youth, Joyce remarked that she could write a book about my childhood.

The seed was planted.

Over the next dozen or so years, Joyce would occasionally bring up the subject but, if I'm honest, I never thought it would go any further and would forever remain an occasional thought in her head.

Again, I was wrong.

As we approached our golden wedding anniversary, Joyce announced that we were going to write the book of my young life.

Now, let me tell you, Joyce is a remarkable woman and when she decides she's going to do something, it gets done, but, as she set to her task, even Joyce did not appreciate the enormity of the project she had committed us to doing.

Thankfully, we had a willing accomplice in Richard Patterson, our friend and neighbour, who joined forces with Joyce to bring my childhood to life using the written word.

Cutting a long story short – which is something that I don't often do, you are now about to read the result of their efforts.

I hope you enjoy it.

Joe

CONTENTS

PROLOGUE

"Joe, Clive is here - he wants to know if you are going out laiking" my Mam shouted. "Okay, I'm coming" I excitedly shouted back.

Running down the steps from my bedroom I dashed straight out to meet Clive, my hurried goodbye still hanging in the air as the door closed behind me. It was a Saturday, so there was no school and, being May, the day was nice and warm.

I'd met Clive the day that I started school and, from that first meeting, we'd formed a bond and took every opportunity to go laiking (playing) together. We were best friends and as close as brothers.

"What do you want to do Joe? We could go and fish in t'beck if we had fishing rods, Maurice and Norman said they had seen trout in Tinkle Beck, shame we haven't any rods" said Clive, looking a bit disappointed.

"We don't need rods, we can tickle them" I announced.

"Tickle them! How do you do that?" Clive looked at me as though I was mad.

"I've never heard of tickling fish to catch them."

"It's easy," I told him. "You just wait until the trout swims under a stone, then you put your hand under the stone and, when you can feel the fish, just tickle its belly. When you think you can hold on to it, grab it round its gills and pull it out of the water."

So off we went down across the field from our farm to Tinkle Beck, two 8 year old boys, chattering away, happy, as ever, just to be in each other's company.

"Just stretch out by the side of the beck and keep quiet, if you make a lot of noise you'll frighten them away" I said in what passed for a loud whisper.

After what seemed like ages, but would probably have been only ten minutes, Clive said he would move further down the beck because he hadn't seen any trout. Just as he moved away I saw one - my heart started beating so fast I thought it would burst through my rib cage. I waited until it swam under a stone, then very quietly I put my hand in to the beck, felt under the stone, found the fish and gently started to tickle it. Confident I'd tickled it enough to calm it, I quickly grabbed it by its gills and pulled it out of the water, throwing it onto the bank before it could slip out of my hands. Was I excited!

It was a big trout, but before I could call out to Clive to tell him, he was shouting me, "Joe, Joe, I'm going to drown! My hand is stuck under a stone and I can't get it out!"

"Don't be daft" I laughed, as I walked over to him.

"You drown if it's your head stuck under the water, not your hand."

I put my hand in to the beck to lift the stone from Clive's hand and, as I lifted it he pulled his hand away - still clutching a very nice brown trout!

"Look at that Joe!" Clive said, smiling all over his face.

"I wasn't going to let go of that, but by gum the water was cold and my shirt sleeve is wet through, but it was worth it".

We compared our trout and decided they were the biggest that had ever been caught.

The afternoon sun was warm on our backs as we proudly carried our catch back to the farm, both of us looking forward to the praise that would undoubtedly come from my Mam when we presented her with our trout.

Not even in my worst nightmares did I think that, just three years later, death and illness would have feasted themselves on the very heart of my family and that I'd have to rely on my fishing and hunting skills just to be able to feed myself.

But I'm already getting way ahead of myself, as my story actually started eight years earlier, during the cold December of the momentous year of 1939. Britain had been at war with Adolf Hitler's Germany for three months when I entered the world, kicking and bawling, into my Mam's strong arms.

1
My Family and Pondhill

Joe Sawley, my dad, was a huge, broad shouldered man. Six foot tall and very well built, even though he was well into his middle years, he was exceptionally strong and able. Given his appearance, on first meeting him, people were often surprised to find that he was of a pleasant mannered disposition. Ask anyone who knew him to describe my Dad and, as well as saying the above, they'd also mention his flat cap, muffler and pipe, which were almost permanent features of his.

Dad worked at John Lunds engineering works at Crosshills, where he was a highly skilled precision engineer and tool maker. He excelled in his craft and was widely acknowledged by both management and his workmates for being a craftsman of the highest calibre.

He worked long hours, which meant he earned good money. You won't be surprised to hear that, in accordance with true Yorkshire tradition, Dad was a bit thrifty. This had allowed him to build up a small nest egg, which he hoped would, one day, allow him to buy a farm of his own.

My Mam, Ada, was a well-rounded woman of medium height, probably overweight, but she said it was good living and you wouldn't argue over that with her! Maybe buxom would best describe Mam. She was strong, hard-working and full of kindness – the sort of person who would give her last penny away. Mam was a home maker, happiest when she was baking and feeding us until we were full to bursting, or as we would call it, brussen. She loved her family and home and would never spend money on herself - not even to have a perm once in a while!

My sister Marjorie, known as Madge, was born three years before me. Mam was 48 when she had me and I think my arrival was a bit of a shock to both her and Dad. My parents were unmarried, meaning both Madge and I were 'born out of wedlock', which in those days was considered to be a sin and was frowned upon.

Mam was, in fact, legally still married to her first husband, to whom she had borne three children, Jack, Denis and Ada. By the time I came along, Jack was already married, Denis had just completed his National Service and Ada was working in the munitions stores. I also had another half-sister, Ethel, who Mam had had when she was 17.

When she'd fallen with Ethel, Mam had expected to marry the lad that she was then courting. He though refused to get married and walked away, leaving Mam pregnant and single, a terrible combination in those days. Ethel's dad had nothing to do with her when she was born and, having joined up, was posted abroad – this being during the First World War. Whilst away fighting, he got injured and lost his sight and so was sent back to England, his war over.

That was when he decided he would marry my Mam after all. Turning up out of the blue and announcing this to her, he was, by all accounts, somewhat taken aback when my mother turned down his generous offer of marriage.

"Tha didn't want to know me or the baby when you could see, but now that you're blind you expect me to marry you and nurse you. Bugger off!"

It seems that my mother had been what you might call a spirited lady from quite a young age.

Whilst having nothing to do with him, Mam did petition the army that they should ensure that he contributed financially to Ethel's upbringing. This was unheard of at the time, but the army, like many others in subsequent years, soon found out that my Mam was not somebody to be messed with. The end result of this was that the army ensured that Ethel's dad contributed to her upkeep financially.

By the time I came along, Ethel was in her thirties, married with a son of her own. As a result, I didn't see much of her, but when we did see her I used to enjoy laiking around with her son Valentine, who spent his childhood pleading with everyone that he met to call him Val.

Nook farm, in Oakworth, was where the family lived at the time of my arrival. Living conditions were very cramped, the floorboards competed to see which could creak the loudest and, the fact that it was rented, all added up to Dad being ever more determined to build up the nest egg, find a small holding in the district and 'own the roof over his head'.

In the spring of 1942 Dad heard of the imminent sale of a small holding at nearby Cowling and, with him having sufficient savings in the bank, managed to place a deposit for a mortgage on the property, which went by the name of Pondhill farm.

Dad was too busy at work to find the time to view Pondhill, but, so determined was he not to miss this chance of owning his own farm, that he was not going to let this small detail stop him. The purchase was completed – little did Joe and Ada realise at the time how many headaches their decision to proceed would cause them.

*

Two months later, we, along with our worldly possessions, were loaded onto a horse and cart and draped in several layers of tarpaulins. We left Oakworth heading for Cowling, a small farming and mill village, where our new home, Pondhill Farm, was waiting for us.

Mam & Dad were full of excitement at the prospect of at long last owning their own home.

Mam, Madge and I were under the tarpaulin sheets, Dad up front driving Polly our old horse on.

"Good lass Polly, we're getting theer" Dad said kindly.

"Ada and ye two kids, don't fall art a t'cart." He calmly advised us.

For two kids of five and two and a half, the trip was a great adventure and, excitedly giggling, we kept peeping out from under the tarpaulin - we seemed to be going on for ever!

All I could see were green fields and stone walls, but Mam was more concerned about everything balanced around us than the fields and walls and kept pulling me back in. "Sit still, you don't want anything falling on you" she gently scolded me.

Then, without warning, Polly stopped suddenly. Our worldly goods gave up the battle they'd been waging with gravity and came tumbling down, some around us and some falling off the cart.

Dad was cursing, but Polly wouldn't move. She started making nervous whinnying noises and had become frightened.

Dad knew what was wrong with her. As we'd neared the farm at the crossroads we were approaching, we had all heard the high pitched squeals. To us kids it just meant we could hear pigs, but what Dad knew that we didn't, was how much horses do not like pigs.

"Bloody pigs" Dad said loudly, as he looked to reassure and calm the horse.

After getting our possessions back onto the cart, Dad again calmly spoke to and comforted Polly, trying to soothe her. Hopeful of having calmed her, he gently coaxed her to plod on once more.

Polly didn't react quite as Dad expected. Without warning, she suddenly set off at a gallop, causing the delicately balanced furniture to move dangerously in the cart, once again defying gravity and doing a crazy dance.

"Gosh Mam, Polly going fast." Five year old Madge giggled, completely unaware of the danger that this posed, both to us and our belongings.

Luckily for us, Polly was an old horse, so didn't gallop for too long before she slowed down to a slow walking pace, allowing the furniture to relax a bit.

From the cart we could once again hear the steady clip-clop, clip-clop of Polly's iron- shod hooves clattering noisily as we travelled along Buckstone road. After passing a few poor hill farms, we reached an old packhorse track, Treacle lane. I found out years later that Treacle Lane had got its name from an erstwhile resident of a nearby cottage, Treacle Billy, who was well known for making treacle puddings.

Our destination, the family's new home, Pondhill Farm, was only a couple of hundred yards away.

2
ARRIVING AT PONDHILL

Polly was a bit weary after the journey from Oakworth, but she plodded up the grass bank to the farm gate. She stopped whilst Dad opened the gate, which was badly in need of repair, then, when she pulled us forward just a few more yards, we could see our new home.

Mam was nearly out of the cart before Dad had pulled Polly to a halt, she was so excited. "Oh Joe, at long last we have got our own farm" she enthused, almost as though until that moment she hadn't dare to believe it was really happening.

Mam and Dad clambered down from the cart and were greeted by a flock of bleating sheep and a dozen or so noisy, wing flapping hens, all running out of the farmhouse's wide open front door, whose well-worn timbers had been cobbled together with an old rope.

With rising trepidation they gingerly entered the farm house, where, for the first time, they took in the grim reality of Pondhill Farm.

Time must have stood still for them, as they just stood and stared in disbelief, until, finally, Mam broke the deafening silence. "Joe, what have we bought?" she uttered, looking very pale.

"Oh Ada, what have I done?" Never before had she heard Dad sound so downhearted.

It was clearly evident to them both that the bleak and broken down moorland farm, located on a wind-blown, heather-clad hillock high above the Summerhouse Clough and beneath the brooding peat moor of Ickornshaw, was in an horrendous state of dilapidation and looking every one of its 200 years.

In the downstairs rooms the damp, worn flag stones were hidden beneath a carpet of sheep droppings and chicken muck that was several inches thick and giving off an extremely offensive reek. Huge, uneven clumps of plaster had fallen off the rough stone walls and most of the window glass was either missing, or broken.

The farm lacked running water, therefore, when needed, water would have to be fetched from a stone trough in the yard, or the nearby spring.

As was commonplace, the call of nature had to be performed in the freezing, dry-stone building out in the yard, probably the home of mice, spiders and other vermin.

The toilet itself consisted of a coarse grained plank, the centre of which had a hole cut out and was perched on top of a stack of stone blocks. When the space beneath the plank became full it had to be emptied by shovelling through the 'muck ole'- an opening at floor level in the back wall of the building, to be scattered as fertiliser on the land.

On a dark winter night, with the wind howling, going to the closet to answer a call of nature was a very terrifying experience.

Dad was upset and angry with himself. How could he have been so daft as to not go and look at the farm properly before he'd put all of his hard-earned money into it?

"I thought t'Nook was grim, but this Pondhill is back o'beyond," Mam thought to herself.

She may have felt extremely dispirited and very downhearted, but being a hard-working, spirited Yorkshire woman and knowing that there was no going back, she wasn't going to let it show in front of my Dad. She'd seen and heard how upset he was and, as ever, was going to support him in any way that she could. She took a deep breath and steadied herself.

"This house is a reet mess, but we can fettle it up. You go and put Polly in the field and leave Young Joe and Madge in the cart for the time being. I'll get the shovels, brush and wheelbarrow from the cart and we'll get stuck in." She announced, turning and heading straight out, so there would be no further discussion.

Going back into the farm house with brushes and shovels, leaving Madge and me wrapped in a blanket in the cart, they set about the horrendous task of cleaning the place up.

"Well, I'd better look upstairs and see what it's like up there," Mam stated as she crossed to the door at the bottom of the staircase.

The door was stuck fast and, no matter how hard Mam pulled, she could not open it, so had to call Dad over to help. Dad pulled hard on it and, after continuing to resist for a few seconds, it gave up the fight against his greater strength and grudgingly opened.

The fortunate effect of the door having been stuck fast was that it had stopped the hens from getting to the bedrooms. Mam looked round and felt a bit better that the upstairs rooms had been spared the fate of those downstairs. That said, everything was still in need of a bloody good cleaning and the small mullioned window panes were all either missing or cracked.

"Joe can remedy the problem by nailing some thick Hessian sacking across the voids as a temporary repair until we can replace the windows, after all at least it's April not winter" she murmured, thinking aloud.

Madge and I had got a bit fed up of sitting in the cart.

"I'm going to see what Mam and Dad are doing" Madge said, scrambling out of the cart. I went to follow but, being small and not yet 3 years old, I fell out of the cart. It was a soft landing on the grass though, so I picked myself up and ran after my sister.

We both entered the farmhouse together and stopped, staring wide-eyed at Dad shovelling this awful smelling muck into a wheelbarrow. Before we could do or say anything Mam shooed us back outside, telling us to play out, but not to go away.

"I don't want the kids in here until it's fettled. If you give me the brush all we need to do initially upstairs is to get rid of the cobwebs and dust. You'll have to put some hessian up over the missing windows, until we can get them fixed. If we get some distemper and colour the walls upstairs, I think it will look nice and Mrs Smith told me that if you put a bit of dolly blue into the distemper you get a nice pale blue shade." Mam was warming to the task in hand, as she relayed her thoughts to Dad.

"Ah, Ada, what have I done bringing you and the kids here to this stinking place? What a bloody mess! I honestly didn't know the farmhouse would be in such a bad state" said Joe quietly, with tear-filled eyes.

"Look here Joe Sawley, we have a roof over our heads, albeit not what we expected. Remember, a lot of folk have been bombed and have nothing and they have lost loved ones, so get on with your shovelling. When I've finished upstairs I'll come and give you a hand down here." Mam, as always, was determined to make the best of things.

"Ada, you are a woman in a million. Any other woman would have run away from this place without a second thought." Dad told her, strength returning to his voice.

"Don't be daft love, it's our home now." and with that, Mam disappeared upstairs, armed with the brush.

*

Mam and Dad were accustomed to hard physical work and soon they had moved thirty wheelbarrow loads of the reeking manure to the other side of the yard, ready to spread on the land at a later date. With the lion's share of the muck clearing task completed, Mam said it was time to have some bait. Calling Madge and me to come over to the cart, she unwrapped the cloth which contained a bit of cheese and some jam and bread. There was also milk for us and a flask of tea for her and Dad.

"By, that tea went down well, Ada, my throat was really dry" Dad said.

"Aye, so was mine" Mam agreed, before adding "Come on Joe, we have to get on. Get your bum off the cart, I want the floors cleaned before Denis and Ada get home from work."

She turned to Madge and me, "You two kids can have a sleep in the cart for an hour - you have been running around all morning."

Just as they were going back to the farm, Mam pointed to the roof.

"Look, Joe, it's got a hole in it!" the frustration was evident in her voice.

"No love, it's only the slates that have blown off. Don't worry, we can soon put them back, but I'll have to get Denis to help me, so it will have to wait until tomorrow." Now it was Dad's turn to do the reassuring.

Mam busied herself sloshing several pails of water, brought in by Dad from the nearby well, over the flagstone floors, then vigorously scrubbing until she could see the colour of the flagstone floor. To the last few pails of water she added pine scented disinfectant. She then got down on her hands and knees and, using old clean rags, wiped away the excess water. Completing the chore, she stood and looked around at what she and Dad had achieved and beamed approvingly.

"I've just got to clean and black-lead the cast Iron range, then you can get a fire going." She smiled at Dad.

"Well, I'll go and nail some hessian sacking up at all the broken windows while you get it ready for me" Dad replied.

Mam, with rolled up sleeves, was busy scraping years of accumulated muck and rust from the Victorian cooking range, which would be relied on for cooking the family's meals, for heating up water and for heating the farmhouse itself.

"By, that range looks like new Ada, you've done a grand job!" Mam beamed at Dad's compliment, as he continued, "I've found some wood and peat in one of the out buildings, so I can get a fire going. If we bring the sofa in, you can fetch the kids in - by they've been good today, neither of them have seemed troubled by today's ordeal."

Madge and me sat on the old horse haired sofa looking around at our new home. "It smells a lot better than before and we won't tell Denis and Ada it was a smelly house Mam" Madge said, knowing her Mam would not want them, or anyone else, to know how bad it had been.

After carrying two huge armfuls of firewood in to the kitchen, Dad set about laying a fire in the grate of the large cast iron range, which was set within a huge fireplace built of rough stone. Dad soon had a roaring fire blazing in the grate. I watched the leaping flames making shadows on the walls and illuminating the sombre surroundings of our home.

As the Pennine night drew in, Dad, working by lighted candle in an old jam jar, attempted to keep out the weather by nailing more hessian sacking to the broken parlour window. Several more candles in jam jars were lit, their flickering yellow light giving a warm comforting glow to the roughly plastered walls.

Mam cooked our first meal on the range - egg on toast! She said it was the best she could muster today, but tomorrow it would be a nice stew.

After Ada and Denis had arrived home and the furniture had all been carried into the house, Mam filled the kettle from the well and made tea. The farmhouse kitchen was soon filled with the warm reassuring glow of the burning wood crackling and spitting in the grate.

We settled down for our first night at Pondhill, still with much anxiety and trepidation about what lay ahead.

3
EARLY DAYS AT PONDHILL

Madge and I shared our parents' bedroom. Ada and Denis each had their own rooms and weren't slow in voicing their opinions of them.

"You couldn't swing a cat round in here!" Denis could be heard shouting.

"This room's so small that this place is worse than t'Nook!" Ada shouted back.

And so it went on, as though the two of them were in competition to see who could complain the most.

Mam was angry with them, she and Dad had worked so hard the day before to get the place clean and all that pair could do was to complain about the rooms being small.

"You have a roof over your head, so shut up nattering and think yourselves lucky!" she said, banging the cast-iron kettle onto the trivet in the fire grate, just in case they were in any doubt as to whether they should shut up or not!

So started our first full day at Pondhill.

Neither Denis, Ada, nor Dad went to work that day. Although it was Saturday, because of the war, work was plentiful and taking the day off would mean losing money that they could ill afford, but making the farm secure and watertight was upmost in Dad's mind. As he would need Denis to assist him to tackle the much needed repairs to the roof, it followed that Denis would have to give up his day's pay.

Meanwhile Ada had ideas of her own

"Let's go down to the Village and see if we can get some distemper to paint the walls in the bedrooms and parlour" she urged.

Mam was reluctant, as she thought the money that they had could be better spent on repairs. White washing the walls could come at a later date, when all the windows had been replaced and she made this point to Ada.

"Oh come on Mam" said Ada, "I'll pay for it out of my wages."

Working at the munitions factory, she earned good money, albeit not on the scale of today's wages. Mam worried about her working there, afraid that the Germans would bomb the factory.

Ada persisted and won, so they set off for Cowling. It was a tidy walk down to the village, out onto Treacle Lane, past Great House and Court House farms, down the hill at Farling Top, arriving on the main road just a few hundred more yards from the village.

When they arrived back about two hours later, both Mam and Ada looked hot and were sweating. In fact, Mam looked in a right flurry, with her face as red as a tomato.

"By 'eck Ada lass, you both look done in. I told you I would tek thee down on horse and cart, it's reet hard wark walking back up yon hill carrying all those tins of distemper." Dad told her, on taking in the sight of the pair of them.

"It's not that, Joe. I heard some folk talking about us in the shop. They didn't know we were behind them." Dad could hear the agitation in Mam's voice as she continued.

"This cheeky, toffee-nosed bitch was saying 'how could a family move into such a horrendously dilapidated place?' and then she said 'I've heard they live over t'brush', but, before I could say anything to them, our Ada told them to mind their own bloody business! Our Ada was reet upset hearing folk talking about us like that."

Dad knew folk would talk, but in a reassuring voice he said "Take no notice, talk's cheap."

Madge, looking up at all of them stood around, said, in a child's innocent voice, "What's living 'over t'brush' mean?"

A long silence followed, with everyone looking at each other, not knowing what to say. Finally, Mam looked at her and said, simply, "It's just a saying about a brush." This satisfied little Madge, who, happy with her answer, went off to play.

Mam and Dad were left feeling a bit bothered, as they both knew that the question would undoubtedly crop up again.

*

Dad, Mam, Denis, and Ada spent every spare hour that summer getting the farm into shape. Everyone knew how important it was to make sure that every draught-hole was blocked up, otherwise we would really suffer when the harsh Yorkshire winter weather swept in off the moors come December.

The seemingly never ending task was made all the harder because of the long working hours that Dad, Denis and Ada were doing in their jobs at the engineering works and the munitions factory. When the three of them arrived home late in the evening they would be exhausted, but Dad would insist on them taking advantage of the light summer nights and spending a couple of hours each night tackling the lengthy list of repairs.

Being young, Ada and Denis wanted to go out with their friends. I remember Mam telling Dad one evening that they wanted to go to the pictures.

"The pictures will have to bloody well wait if we are going to keep warm this winter!" he answered, in a tone that said that the subject was not open to discussion.

Mam knew that working so hard was taking a toll on everyone and that Dad would not have spoken so sharply if he hadn't been so tired, but she also knew that Dad still felt guilty about purchasing the farm without realising how run down and neglected it was and that he was driven to get it into a fit state for the family to live in.

Slowly, the back breaking days turned into weeks, which, in turn, painfully turned into months. The repairs on the list were ticked off one by one, with plaster put back on the walls and mullion windows replaced, room by room. As the repairs were completed to each room, Mam and Ada turned their attention to making the place more homely, with Ada applying whitewash to the walls and Mam making a tab rug.

The farm had 28 acres of land, but, like all Yorkshire hill farms, the land was poor with small sloping fields divided by dry-stone walls. Like the rest of the farm, these walls had been left to fall into disrepair and the constant battering from the harsh Yorkshire wind, coupled with the unwanted attention of the roaming, hardy, moorland sheep, meant that most of the walls were knocked down in several places.

Even though some of the dry-stone walls divided the property from the next farm, Dad had decided that their repair could wait until after the farm house was put in order, after all, he'd reasoned, we didn't yet have any stock, so it didn't matter.

It wasn't long, though, until our first animals were introduced to Pondhill.

Dad had been asked by the local poultry farmer to do a few small engineering jobs and, after a bit of bartering, he agreed that these would form part payment for some pullets. Having kept the details of the deal he had struck secret, Mam was surprised to see him arrive home one day accompanied by two dozen point-of-lay pullets. Luckily, the hen hut left by the previous owner had fared better than the farmhouse itself and all it needed was a little sawdust on the floor and the perch made secure for the pullets to roost on.

Mam was over the moon and was soon telling Dad how she would sell the eggs. Dad laughed and said, "Ada lass, at least wait until hens start laying."

Every morning Mam went to feed the hens and look for eggs, until one morning we heard a cry of delight and looked out to see her hurrying back up to the house, arms aloft, with each hand holding a freshly laid egg.

They were happy days for me. I was still too young to have started school, so spent my days playing and 'helping' my Mam, whose day on the farm was always busy from morning until night.

I paid great attention to whatever Mam was doing and she, in turn, patiently explained what she was doing, how she did it and why she was doing it. Without realising it at the time, I gained an awful lot of practical knowledge from my Mam that would prove invaluable to me a few years later, when the situation would change and my life would become unrecognisable compared to what it had been.

The lessons I learned by watching my Mam and Dad, along with the determination and work ethic that I also inherited from them were to become vital to my very survival.

I didn't though realise any of that at that time and was just happy to spend my days with the mother that I adored.

My favourite day was baking day, when the smell of the buns and apple pies baking in the oven filled the house and made me feel hungry. I knew I would get a treat of a freshly baked bun and would wait impatiently for them to cook. Even better than this though was my treat when Mam had finished baking - she'd let me lick the big mixing bowl out! Eh, the bowl was nearly as big as me and I remember getting my head right inside it and licking it until nothing was left, apart from a few bits on my nose and around my mouth. After that I would sit on Mam's knee while she gave me a big cuddle, making me feeling safe and warm, as we waited until it was time for the rest of the baking to come out of the oven.

4
PONDHILL BECOMES A FARM AGAIN

After a year living at Pondhill, a long year full of hard work, sweat and more than a few thoughts of 'what have we done', the farm house was finally taking shape. Well, nearly! It was nearly draught proof, with the small mullioned windows having been replaced and the kitchen and parlour were nearly done, with the walls roughly plastered and white washed. Dad decided that 'nearly' would have to do and that it was time to turn attention to the farm itself.

Dad wanted to get the farm into shape as soon as he could, for two reasons. Firstly, the farm needed to start 'providing' for the family. He knew that this needed to happen sooner rather than later, so was keen to get stock onto the land as soon as possible. Secondly, and more urgently, Mam had started a vegetable patch and was bending his ear constantly about neighbouring sheep stealing her veg!

Dad and Denis set to the task of rebuilding the dry-stone walls round the farm. As with the rest of the farm, the walls that were meant to border the fields had been left to fend for themselves and, over the years, they had lost their fight against the ravages of the Yorkshire weather. The extent of their collapse was such that even the most optimistic person could no longer describe them as walls. Amongst other problems, this meant that the sheep from neighbouring farms could wander onto Pondhill whenever they liked, and help themselves to the fresh vegetables growing on the vegetable patch that Mam had established.

Building a dry stone wall is a much underrated skill which Yorkshire men have taught their sons through countless generations. Even today it is a skill that is much admired, with competitions to find the best 'waller' held at each country show. It is generally considered that a well-built dry stone wall is a work of art. Suffice to say that Dad and Dennis weren't artists! They would have won awards for effort, enduring weeks of aching muscles and joints and each giving gallons of sweat for the cause, but as for the result of their labours – well, the walls might have stopped a cow, but a rabbit could run through at will!

Life for everyone consisted of long days full of hard work. The Second World War was still raging and food and clothing were rationed. Even when our ration books allowed us to get some clothes, we couldn't, as they were too expensive. So, as happened in many other families, our Mam made sure that every item of clothing was used to the maximum. When one of us outgrew something, it was handed down to the next of us. Everything had a use. Even when something was worn and torn beyond repair, it was used to make patches for running repairs to something else. Nothing was wasted. When I think about how much effort is made nowadays, to try and get people to recycle things – I tell you, our parents were ahead of their time!

In those early, pre-school years, I didn't give a second thought that all my clothes were hand downs, patched and cut down to make them fit. Girls though have, right through history, liked to look pretty, so it was harder for Madge and Ada. They didn't complain about it a lot, but every now and then one or other of them would have a moan about it to Mam and, each time they did, Mam would look at them sympathetically and say "We ain't got posh clothes, but we have food in our bellies."

For all Mam was a strong, hardy woman, who made sure that what money we did have was spent on what was needed and not 'wasted' buying new clothes when she could alter and patch what we already had, she was also proud. Our clothes may have been altered, patched and repaired, but they were always clean.

Finally, after many weeks of back breaking work, the stone walling was sufficiently complete both to secure Mam's vegetables and to be stock proof. For all that Dad, Denis and Ada were all working, the on-going refurbishment of the farm and farm house, along with the cost of putting food on the table, meant that there was little spare money. Dad knew that it was a catch 22 situation – for the farm to start providing for his family it had to be stocked, but providing for the family in the meantime meant there was little money to invest in stock. Despite the fact that he already had no spare time, Dad looked for any extra work that he could find and soon found some with a local farmer.

One day, soon after, Dad arrived home with a cow walking in front of him.

"Joe, what are you doing with that cow?" Mam asked him.

"It's a present for you, Ada" he told her.

Mam was speechless, "But, but, how did you get it?" she stammered.

"Well, I've been doing work down at Brown's farm and I saw he had some nice young heifers and I thought to myself 'my Ada would like one of them', so with the pay from him and a little bit of cash, we did a deal. We both know that it's time we had stock in the fields."

Mam's brain began working nineteen to the dozen, with her tongue not far behind. "We can have milk, butter, cheese and cream …" the words came speeding out of her mouth.

"Steady Ada love, let's put her in t'mistal and see if you can remember how to milk her," Dad chuckled.

The heifer was a small brown and white short horn and by the time they'd settled her in the mistal (cow shed), Mam had named her Mary. Mam soon got the knack of milking her and, in no time at all, had turned her hand to making butter and cheese.

The first time she made butter and cheese she called us all to the table at tea time. I remember we were all sat there and Mam proudly brought out the bread, butter and cheese.

"Now then, try that!" she said, watching us intently, waiting for our response.

"By Ada love, that's the best tasting butter and cheese I've ever had." Dad soon announced and, as we all voiced our agreement, our Mam smiled contentedly, enjoying the compliment. Little did we realise it, as we all sat there that day happily munching away, but that was the start of Mam's little business.

Word soon got round that Mam had a few potatoes, veg, eggs, butter and cheese to trade with and people soon started calling. Some bought goods for cash, whilst others would hand over ration coupons, which were as useful a form of currency as cash in those days, in exchange for the produce. Mam was happy to deal in either currency and was even known to trade her food for other 'products' – us kids regularly got some 'new' clothes that some other family had outgrown. Trade was good and Mam was kept busy.

*

One day in late summer, me and Madge, who had just got home from school, could see that Mam was impatient for Dad, Denis and Ada, to get home from work. Finally, they approached the farm house. As they stepped through the door Dad made a point of exaggeratedly sniffing the air, following this by saying loudly "Eeh Ada lass, thee tea does smell reet grand".

"All that I could get from t'butcher was a bit o'scrag-end of mutton. Ah've dug up some spuds from t'garden, so we'll be hevin' a reet tasty stew." said Mam, breaking into a smile.

"Now, everyone come to the table." she hurriedly continued. We had a big pine table in the kitchen, which we all sat round for our meals, and today Mam was rushing everyone to sit down.

"What's up Ada? What's rush?" Dad asked.

"I've somet to tell you." she replied.

"Eeh, Ada, thee'r not!!" Dad had suddenly lost some colour.

"No, you daft fool," Mam shot quickly back, "sit down and I'll tell you."

Mam had everyone's attention and was smiling like the Cheshire Cat. With her audience in place she was finally able to tell the tale that she'd been desperate to share all afternoon.

"Who do you think came t'farm today, wanting to buy some butter and cheese?" she began, asking a question but not wanting, or waiting for, an answer.

"I'll tell you," she continued, "That cheeky, toffee- nosed bitch, who'd said that day in the shop, 'how can anyone live in a place like Pondhill' and that we lived over t'brush. Well, I was a bit flummoxed when I saw her, but before I could say anything she called me 'Mrs Sawley'…" the words were spilling out of her, but, before she could go on, Denis interrupted her.

"You should have told her to bugger off." he said, with Ada immediately voicing her agreement with him.

"Oh no," Mam told them "I sold her some butter." her face was beaming as she continued triumphantly "And charged her one shilling more than anyone else!"

Everyone laughed and congratulated Mam. I didn't really understand what was going on, but laughed because everyone else was, and besides, I was happy because I could see that Mam was very pleased with herself.

5
FAMILY LIFE PRE-SCHOOL

With the farm up and running, life settled into a familiar pattern. Whilst Dad, Denis and Ada were at work and Madge was at school, Mam would be busy making and trading her produce, ably assisted of course by me. After work had finished, the men would continue with the never-ending list of jobs around the farm, whilst Mam and Ada would prepare dinner and clear up afterwards.

A typical evening would then see us sat by the range, as Mam repaired, altered, or patched clothes. I think that sometimes Mam must have felt all but defeated by the problem of keeping all of the family clothed. She was thankful for any garment that anyone would give her for us, be it second hand or even third hand, regardless of fit or suitability. Night after night she would sit repairing, altering and patching garments, with only an oil lamp or candle for light. Dad would say "nay Ada love, you can't wark in this poor leet, it'll do your eyes in," but Mam would just smile up at him and carry on.

Sunday night was bath night at Pondhill and Dad would lift the big galvanised tin bath from where it was hung on a hook in the back wash kitchen and place it in front of the range.

I used to like helping Dad to bring in several buckets of cold water from the well and tipping them in the bath. Mam would boil water in the large iron kettle on the hob, adding it to the bath water until the temperature was just about aired. She would then place the clothes horse, covered with blankets and towels, around the tin bath, to allow Madge to bathe in privacy.

Madge always wanted to go in to the bath first, because she said that when I got in I peed in the bath. I used to protest that I didn't, but Madge always said that she knew I did, because she could see the bubbles in the bath water. She wasn't daft, our Madge.

With Madge stating her accusations and me protesting my innocence, Mam would tell us both to go out to the closet before we got in the tin bath. This would have Madge and me joining forces and whining about it being too cold to go outside, until Mam would shut off our protests by telling us to have a pee in the bucket in the back kitchen. This was as exciting to us kids as having a bath was and was all part of the ritual of bath night. We'd be giggling as we peed in the bucket, as Mam closed out this part of the ritual by gently warning us, "Dad and me have to get in the bath after you two, so I mean it - no peeing in the bath."

That is how it was; with us all sharing the same bath water. Mam or Dad would keep boiling up the kettle to top up the bath water and keep it aired, whilst Madge, then me, then Mam and finally Dad would take our turn in the ever darkening water.

Bath time over, we would all sit in front of the range smelling of carbolic soap, Mam and Dad drinking tea, Madge and me drinking hot milk.

So as not to waste the bath water, after we'd all finished, Mam would put all the family's dirty clothes into the bath and leave them there, soaking, until the following day. Monday was her wash day and, as she scooped the clothes into the bath Mam would remind us all "Hot water, no matter how dirty, is not to be wasted, particularly when you've had to carry it from the well and then used fuel on the fire to boil it."

Whilst our clothes had all lived several lives before we got them, Mam always insisted that we had something warm and hard wearing on our feet, so one thing that we did get new were made to measure clogs.

Clogs were made with leather uppers nailed to a strong wooden sole. Men's clogs had iron rims nailed round the edge of the wooden soles and heels, so that the wooden sole didn't wear, whereas ladies clogs had rubber instead of iron rims. The mill workers and farmers needed cheap, hard wearing footwear which would protect their feet and keep them relatively comfortable and clogs fitted the bill.

With the day that I was to start school approaching, Mam took me down to see the local clogger, Sidney Pass. His shop, I remember, was down Winkholme lane, which was on the way to school, down in the village. Sidney made and sold clogs to all the farmers and mill workers, male and female.

"Now Sidney," Mam announced, "I want a pair of clogs for young Joe, with irons on the wooden soles and room to grow into."

Sidney got out his tape measure, pencil and paper and proceeded to measure my feet. I don't know why he bothered, even at that age I knew that Mam would insist that they be made two sizes too big!

With the measurements written down he told Mam that they would be ready in a week.

6
My First Day At School

All summer long I'd known what was coming up – the day that I had to start school. When the day finally arrived I felt excited, but a bit scared. Mam kept telling me not to be frightened, because Madge was at the same school and would keep an eye on me. It didn't matter how many times she said it, I was still a bit scared.

My clothes for school consisted of a wool jumper, which had been darned with so many different colours of wool it must have looked like Joseph's coat of many colours; my short pants, which actually hung to well below my knees; and wool stockings, which insisted on falling into my new clogs, no matter how often, or how tight, I pulled them up.

When I got dressed that first morning for school, I didn't give a single thought to what my clothes looked like. After all, I had never had new clothes, so had never known any different and, besides, living on the farm, having second hand, repaired clothes had never mattered.

The first thing school taught me was that, to a lot of people, it did matter.

But, as I said, what my clothes looked like was the last thing on my mind when I got dressed that morning. I was so happy when I put on my new clogs, that I had to keep looking at them. Black leather tops with brass rimes fastening the leather tops to the wooden soles, plus the iron rims on the wooden soles. I thought they were fantastic.

I clattered all around the kitchen, again and again, until Mam couldn't stand the racket anymore and told me to stop. In all the ex-

28

citement of trying out my new clogs I forgot that I was meant to be a bit scared!

Soon enough it was time to go, so, with me holding on to both Mam and Madge's hands, we set off to walk to school. Maurice Jackson, who lived a bit further down the road from Pondhill, at Court House farm, had started school six months before me. He was coming out of the farm gate just as we passed by, so joined us in the walk to school.

It was a long walk down to the school - out of Treacle Lane, down Oakworth road passing the Mill cottages at Farling Top, before crossing the main road and entering Winkholme Lane, from where we could see through the village to the church and beyond, to the school that had served the village since 1875.

Maurice and I chatted away, hardly pausing for breath, but all the while my mind was wondering more and more about what school would be like. When we crossed the main road and entered Winkholme Lane and I got my first look at the school, all I could see was a very large, dark building, complete with big iron gates. My excitement drained quickly and a knot of dread quickly started forming in my gut - it was not a welcoming sight for a 5 year old boy who'd barely been off his farm.

Even though the knot inside me was growing, I couldn't tear my gaze away, so just kept staring at the school as my legs brought it ever closer to me. The spell was broken when I heard our Madge calling out to someone. I looked round and saw that she was calling to her friend Vera Lumb, who was standing talking to Doreen Paley, who was with her Mam and her little brother.

As my mam and Mrs Paley exchanged greetings and chatted, I looked again at Doreen's little brother. He was stood there looking as dejected and forlorn as me. I shuffled round in front of him, said hello and told him my name. When he replied and told me his name, little did either of us know that we would share a friendship that would last over sixty five years and would only be broken by death.

"Are you starting school today as well?" I asked.

"I am, but I don't like the look of it!" Clive informed me.

"Me neither" I agreed, "But we have to go, we're not allowed to stay home."

Clive was a very small lad with fair hair. Like me, he wore patched, handed down jumper and pants. Mam said he looked as if he needed feeding up, but he was as tough as old boots, as I found out later when we got into fights with other kids.

All of a sudden the air was filled with a repetitive clanging noise that stopped all conversation. The school bell had announced that it was time to go into the classroom. Me and Clive said our goodbye's to our Mams and nervously went in to school. Shepherded into the infants' classroom, we automatically looked for two seats next to each other and readied ourselves for whatever was to come.

Our first day at school went off very well. Mrs Walsh, our teacher, was very kind, didn't look down her nose at us because we had patched clothes and, even better, she smelt very nice! She read stories to us and there were lots of coloured crayons to draw with. Then Mrs Walsh got us to count out the numbers on the blackboard, which, to Clive's amazement, I found easy.

"How do you know about numbers and counting?" asked Clive, who, like the other new kids, had stayed silent when Mrs Walsh had asked us to count out loud.

"I count the hens at home with me mam" I told him.

At play time I laiked in the playground with my new found mates Clive and Maurice. Me and Clive decided school was going to be alright, so we would come again in the morning!

At the end of a memorable first day at school, Maurice, Madge, and I trekked happily back home. Mam was waiting for us when we got there and, sweeping me up in her arms and giving me a cuddle, said "Ah've missed thee, young Joe."

That evening I told everyone all about Mrs Walsh, all about what we did at school and all about Clive, my new friend. I told them that school was alright, but that school dinners weren't half as good as Mam's!

When I'd finally finished telling everyone all my exciting news, Dad put a large cardboard box on the kitchen table and told Mam that it was a present for her. She opened it to reveal a wireless set, powered by two accumulator batteries.

"Oh Joe love, I'm over the moon. What a fantastic present." Mam said, smiling.

"Well love, you being on your own now young Joe's at school, I thought it would be a bit a' company for you."

So that night, sat in the warmth round the fire in the kitchen, we enjoyed listening to the news and music on the wireless. We all agreed that the wireless was great – apart from one small problem. The trouble was that once the accumulator batteries had drained they had to be carried down to Walter Brigg's garage in Cowling for recharging. No-one was quick to volunteer for the job of carrying two heavy batteries down to the village. How things have changed in the last sixty years - kids of today wouldn't know how to use a wireless run by accumulator batteries, in fact I don't even think they would know what an accumulator was!

7
THE SCHOOL SUMMER HOLIDAY

The first year in school flew by and, almost as soon as it had started, it was coming to an end. The summer term was over and the school would be closed for the 4 week summer holiday.

Norman Binns was a local lad who was three years older than me. Because of the age difference, when he was at school he would laike with the older kids, but at weekends and during school holidays he would hang out with us when he could. I say when he could, because he often had to help his Dad on their farm, 'Dean Field'. Norman was a big strapping lad, with a deep, booming voice just like his Dad, Mr Binns, who was known to everyone as 'Big Norman'.

This particular day, at the beginning of the school holidays, Big Norman was taking us up to Ickornshaw moor, to dig for peat. As well as Big Norman, there was Norman, my friend Maurice and me. We all climbed onto the horse and cart, each carrying our lunch of cheese and bread. None of us took anything to drink, as we would just use the stream on the moor.

We set off and soon passed Cuckoo Rock, just before we started to climb up to the moor. Cuckoo Rock got its name because every year a cuckoo would return to the same spot and would land on the rock. We were playing our usual game, seeing who could hear the cuckoo first, when Big Norman told us all to get off the cart and walk up the hill. Big Norman was not going to have his horse tired before it started working.

It was a long pull up onto the moor and the track was just a rough mud track. Every so often the horse would slip, giving all of us a scare each time that it did. Suddenly, without warning the horse suddenly stopped dead in its tracks.

"What's up with the horse Mr Binns?" we all asked.

"It's having a piss. It always stops here for a piss" Big Norman informed us, in a matter of fact way.

As we three lads were still laughing, the horse unhurriedly finished its toilet and, only then, continued on its way.

It's hard work digging peat out of the ground. First, you cut the peat into slabs and then build it up into big mounds, so the wind could dry it. If the peat wasn't dry when you brought it off the moor, then it would not burn on the fire. As the day wore on, Norman and his Dad carried on digging out more peat, whilst Maurice and I were filling the cart with the wind dried peat.

The peat was fuel for winter, so we all knew how important it was to dig as much as we could. I knew half of this load would be going to Pondhill, so I was putting as much as I could onto the cart.

Maurice said "I think we have got a big load Joe, the poor horse will be buggered."

I shook my head at him as I replied, "Don't be daft, Maurice; it's all downhill going back."

It was late in the afternoon before we all got on the cart and set off for home. Big Norman was walking in front of the cart, to steady the horse as it was going down the hill. I was very tired and very dirty, but I knew that my work wasn't yet finished, for when we got back home half of the load would have to be stacked in one of the Pondhill out buildings.

As, finally, Big Norman pulled the horse to a stop at Pondhill, Denis and Ada were waiting to help with our half of the load. I don't think I'd ever been so glad to see them.

Whilst everyone looked at the stack of peat and said how well we had done, Mam took one look at me and sent me off to wash my hands and face in the well.

Next Morning, Clive came over to see me. Mam said she wanted us to go up on the moor and pick some bilberries, which was a lot easier than digging for peat. So off we went, chattering away about everything and nothing as we walked up the hill to the moor. Picking the bilberries was easy, but, for all that we picked loads, after we'd walked all the way back to Pondhill, we only had a jam jar full to give to Mam. As she took in the sight of blue skin around both of our mouths, Mam didn't have to ask what had happened to the rest of what we'd picked. Mam knew that we'd handed over enough bilberries for her to make a pie, so wasn't cross that we'd eaten most of what we'd picked.

Still smiling at the sight in front of her, Mam then announced to us that Mrs Brown had asked if Joe & Clive would like to pick some bilberries for her and that Mam had told her that we would.

"Aw Mam, we have just walked up to the moor and back" I protested.

"Well, you have nothing better to do, so go back and pick some bilberries for Mrs Brown."

Mam's reply was accompanied by a look that said that that was the end of the discussion. Grudgingly we set off for the moor again.

"Flipping heck, Joe, we landed right in that" Clive muttered.

"Didn't we just" I sullenly agreed, as we continued our long trek to the moor, grumbling all the way.

Once at the moor we again started picking bilberries, but this time with little appetite for the task. After what seemed like ages at the time, but was probably no more than ten or fifteen minutes and, still lacking any enthusiasm, we came up with a plan.

"I know," I turned to Clive, my voice suddenly filled with enthusiasm, "let's put a few sheep turds in with the bilberries. It will help to fill the jam jar and I don't think she'll notice, because I think she can't see very well!"

"Brilliant idea" said Clive.

So that's exactly what we did and it was two much happier boys who made the return journey from the moor a little later.

We did feel guilty though; when Mrs Brown said how good we had been to pick bilberries for her and gave us each a penny. I often wonder if she enjoyed her pie.

*

I didn't laik with Clive a lot in the summer holidays, as he lived up Cowling Hill at the Mount and it was a long walk for both of us, whether he walked to Pondhill, or I walked up Cowling Hill. I know he did like coming to our farm though, because Mam always fed him well!

As the summer holidays continued, Norman, Maurice and some of the kids from the village would come to swim and play in Tinkler Beck. We would bank it up with sods to make it a bit deeper, so that we could swim in it.

I liked laiking in the beck, but the problem was I didn't have any swimming trunks, so, the first day that all the lads were there, I ran home and asked Mam if she could find me something to swim in. Knowing my Mam, I knew that she would find me something. She did - a pair of Madge's white, silk knickers!

Off I ran back to the beck in my new swimming trunks.

We were all jumping into the water, which was freezing. Being kids, at first we didn't feel the cold, or, at least, didn't care about it, so we were all laughing and shouting and having a great time. The freezing water wasn't going to be ignored though and, after a good while, we did all begin to turn blue and feel a bit cold, so we got out and lay on the grass bank to dry off.

Everyone started to laugh and, at first, I couldn't work out what it was that they were laughing at. Then I looked down and saw that my soaking wet silk knickers were totally transparent, showing everything distinctly and hiding nothing!

I tried to cover my embarrassment, as Norman and Maurice shouted "we can see Joe Sawley's willy and bum!"

I ran home in tears, unable to stop the shouts and laughter of the other kids, which still echoed around my head long after I was out of earshot.

Mam said she would buy me some proper swimming trunks.

All of our summer holidays were spent at home. We never had holidays at the seaside, but we never thought about it, after all, what you hadn't had you didn't miss and I loved the holidays because I got to laik with my mates every day.

One day, Norman, Maurice and me decided we wanted a gang hut. We decided that the old hen house at Pondhill would be perfect, especially as, because of where it was positioned, no-one could see it from the farm.

Dad said we could have it to play in. I think both him and Mam thought that it would keep us out of mischief. How wrong they were.

The hen house needed a lot of repair, the north facing side in particular had borne the brunt of the rain and harsh weather and its wood was completely rotten. Undeterred by the task before us, we set about finding bits of wood to use to fix it. It took ages, but, after days of hard work, at last we all stood there and looked upon our gang hut. As everyone knows though, a gang hut isn't a gang hut if it hasn't got a name, so the three of us turned our thoughts to what our gang and hut should be called.

After a lot of discussion and argument, we decided that the name would be Saw for me, Bin for Norman, and Jack for Maurice Jackson. The "Sawbinjack" gang hut was christened.

Now, Sawbinjack had to be furnished. We all agreed that we needed something to sit on, but the thing was, in those days, not a lot got thrown away. This thought didn't put us off though, because there was one place that we knew that never let us down, no matter what we needed. It was like our very own department store, with an endless supply of stock. Chattering away about what we needed for Sawbin-jack we headed up to the tip.

Searching the tip was a very dirty and smelly job, but we didn't mind. As ever, the tip didn't let us down and we soon found just what we were looking for. Our three piece suite was grand. The first part was a wooden chair and we all decided that the missing leg wasn't a problem, as we could soon find a piece of wood and make a replacement. Another wooden chair was part two, and, whilst this one had no back, the legs and seat were sound. Our suite was completed by our settee, two large stones with a plank of wood placed between them.

Our gang hut was now ready for our first meeting.

Now, I'm sure you know that gang meetings have to be secret, so when the three of us gathered inside Sawbinjack, we shut the door behind us. The only thing was, as it was summer and we were sitting inside a hen hut, on a hot day, with the door closed, we all nearly suffocated. Not content with nearly suffocating through the heat, I had picked up some tab ends which Denis had left in the ashtray in the kitchen and taken them to the gang hut. Maurice had brought a single match and we huddled together, each with a tab end clamped in our teeth, to make sure we got all three lit.

As none of us had smoked before, we chatted about how we'd seen others do it and decided that to smoke you had to take a deep breath, get the smoke in your mouth and then blow it out.

It didn't work.

We coughed and spluttered and felt sick, until, at last, I got enough breath back to speak. "Flipping heck! I don't think that's what you do, it never made our Denis sick." I told my choking friends.

For the next few years, Sawbinjack became a meeting place for our mates from the village. We would talk, argue and fall out, but always got back to being friends. Sadly, our horrific first attempt at smoking didn't put us off and, looking back, the gang hut became a smoking den.

As well as being used for smoking, the Sawbinjack cabin was used for conjuring up what we should do next. One of the things we would sometimes decide was to go and torment Curly Blackburn.

Curly lived by himself at Dean Hall farm and, on one such occasion, Maurice, Norman and me, made our way there with mischief in mind. When we got to the farm, we looked through the window and saw that Curly was inside, sat in front of the fire.

"Let's put some sods on top of his chimney pot and see what happens," one of us suggested.

We picked up some sods, climbed quietly onto the roof and placed them so that the chimney pot was covered. Trying to stifle our giggles, we climbed down and crept round to look through his window, so that we could see his reaction.

As the room filled with smoke, he started to cough and splutter, just as we'd imagined. The three of us were in fits of laughter as we watched. Our laughter soon stopped though, as his next reaction was something we hadn't even considered.

The door opened and Curly came running out with his gun.

The sound of the gunshot was ringing in the air around us, as we heard Curly shout "I'll kill you young buggers if you come up here again!"

We ran all the way back to the cabin, puffing and sweating. Beads of sweat had run down Norman's face and misted up his glasses.

"He could have killed us!" Norman gasped. It was an effort for him to speak at all, he was so breathless, but he carried on, "I'm not going up there again, I nearly shit my pants when I saw the gun!"

Our visits to Joe, at Higher Dean Farm, were far more enjoyable. For a start, he didn't have a gun. His farm was way out in the middle of the moor, but it was worth the long trek to listen to the stories that he told us about his life.

As young boys, we all thought that he lived in the cellar. It wasn't really the cellar, it was the first storey of a three storey farm house, which you could enter through a small door at the bottom of the building.

We would sit there in the candle light and listen, spellbound, as he told us his stories. We forgot the time, because we were so engrossed in the tales that he would tell us. Sometimes, he would tell a story that scared us near to death and, afterwards, when we were walking home across the moor late at night, every sheep that made a noise was a ghost.

Despite being scared witless, we would go back time and time again. This was our entertainment when we were kids, listening to the old folk telling stories.

8
BACK TO SCHOOL

All too soon the school holidays came to an end. I was looking forward to going back to school, where I would have a new teacher, a different classroom and, best of all, I would get to see my best friend Clive every day. The only sad thought that I had about going back to school was that Mrs Walsh wouldn't be teaching us again.

So, overall I was in a happy mood as Madge and I set off for school. On the way down we met Norman and Maurice and the four of us walked happily down together. My mood improved still further when we reached the school gates and met up with Clive. We were both chattering away to each other about the school holidays as we walked into the school and entered our new classroom.

"Who is making that noise?" shouted our new teacher Mrs Scott.

"Crikey," I thought, "we haven't even sat down yet."

Mrs Scott was glaring at me as she demanded "What's your name?"

"Joe Sawley"

"And yours?" she turned her gaze to Clive as she spoke.

"Clive Paley, miss."

As she continued to stare down at us, Mrs Scott continued, "Well, sit down and don't speak unless you are spoken to."

No sooner had I whispered "Clive, I don't think I'm going to like this teacher," than I was hit with a book round my head.

Her voice made its way into my head, despite the sudden ringing in my ear.

"I said no talking!"

"Mam at Pondhill, with a young me just visible in the background."

"Dad, with his ever-present pipe and cap"

"Pondhill in the early 1940's, after we'd made it habitable"

"Mam and me, when I was still young enough to be cute!"

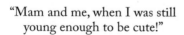

"Me and Madge, after we'd been digging peat"

"Yours truly, aged 11. What a handsome chap!"

"The Yorkshire Moors – my playground"

"My best mate, Clive"

"My other best mates, Maurice and
Norman"

"Ada at Pondhill, around the
mid 1940's"

"Denis, taken during his National Service"

During the war years times were obviously extremely difficult and, across the country, teaching methods were strict, with harsh forms of discipline readily dished out. When I looked at Mrs Scott I saw a fat, ugly woman with a great big wart on her face, no wonder she was able to scare all of us kids before she even opened her mouth.

As well as this, I soon decided that our teacher was a snob. She did little to disguise what she thought of runny-nosed, raggedy kids like Clive and me, giving the appearance of being disgusted by us, as though we could contaminate her. Her attitude to each child depended on their circumstances. For those few clean, tidy kids, whose parents had shops in the village, she had all the time in the world. By comparison, she begrudged every second that she had to spend dealing with the farmers' kids, who probably smelled of cow muck.

Given the above, it came as no surprise that Clive and I were singled out to be "slop monitors".

Being a slop monitor was a really smelly job that no one ever volunteered to do. It involved collecting all of the waste food left over from the school dinners and ladling it into galvanised pails. When full, these had to be delivered to the pig farm for feeding to the pigs.

A dirty and smelly job it may have been, but Clive and I didn't mind it at all, because it got us out of the classroom and away from Mrs Scott.

After we'd filled the pails, we would each carry two buckets of slops and walk over to John Willy's pig sties in Ickornshaw. The galvanised pails were quite big and, when full of slops, were really heavy. These days, nobody would expect kids of 6 and 7 years old to carry a bucket that heavy, but we had to carry two each over the half mile distance to the pig sties.

John Willy was a great big genial character, who suffered from lameness. If the slops buckets were full to the top and we hadn't spilt any he would give us each a penny and we would rush over to Mrs Emmot's grocers shop in Ickornshaw. Mrs Emmot stocked anything that she thought she would be able to sell, even keeping animal feeds and paraffin in the flat above the shop and, because of this, there was always a strange, strong smell in the shop. Not that we were bothered by it. We'd rush in and buy gobstoppers, liquorice sticks, or anything else that they had for a penny.

Whatever the weather, we carried out the smelly slops work every school day.

As well as our daily slop duties, during the winter months Clive and I were also made to help with stoking the boiler that fed the school's central heating. If the boiler man wasn't there we had to stoke the boiler and, even if he was there, if there was a delivery of cinders then we had to help him unloading all of the cinder sacks.

At the time, me and Clive didn't mind having to do these jobs, again, both of us happy to do anything that got us out of the classroom and away from Mrs Scott. Looking back though, it's hard to believe that it was allowed to happen. Can you imagine any child aged 6 or 7 being told to help the boiler man today? As kids we didn't realise it, but it was a very dangerous job for two young lads. We had to open the door of the boiler, which itself was very hot, then shovel cinders in through the door. When the wet cinders hit the hot embers black smoke would rush out of the door and we had to jump back just to avoid the worst of it.

Arriving home after school on the days we had been in the boiler house, my face, hands and clothes were absolutely filthy and Mam would want to know what I had been up to. I never did tell her. I knew that she would have gone straight to the school and made sure that we never had to do it again and, as hard and dirty as it was, working in the boiler house was a lot better than being in Mrs Scott's class!

We got a few good cloutings round the ear from Mrs Scott, who would often go into a tantrum whilst she was taking the class. All of us kids knew when a tantrum was about to start, with the slightest misdemeanour, real or unintended, capable of setting her off.

It was quite a sight.

Forms and desks would topple over as she dragged us out, clouting us round the ears with one hand and throwing our exercise books in the air with her other hand, so that pages were flying all over the class-room. For those girls with plaits in their hair, it was bad news. Mrs Scott would drag you out with your hair to the front of the class, or bang your head on the desk, so for the girls with plaits she could get a really good grip.

She never favoured anyone, well, only the shopkeepers' kids. It was like a hurricane when she was in a bad mood. Clive and me tried to keep our heads down, but it never worked and we always got a whack around our heads or across our backs.

Somehow, every weekend, having survived another week in class, we were able to forget about Mrs Scott for two days.

9
DAD BRINGS HOME THE BACON

One day, Dad purchased a large sow and, not long after, I heard him telling Mam that he would have to get Mr Binns to bring his boar over to brim her. I didn't know what they meant, so I asked Clive. He didn't know either, but we decided that, whatever it was, it sounded exciting. I'd heard Dad saying that the boar was coming on Saturday, so me and Clive decided that we'd be there to watch whatever it was that was going to happen.

Saturday morning soon came and Madge joined Clive and I to watch whatever 'brimming' involved. We didn't have to wait long before Mr Binns arrived, walking behind this huge boar with massive curved tusks. Madge, Clive and me looked on in amusement at the sight of this huge boar.

"What's it going to do?" I asked.

In reply Clive just sat staring at the boar and Madge started to giggle. I don't know whether she heard Madge giggling, or whether it was just coincidence, but before any of us could say or do anything else Mam came out and shouted over to us.

"Come Inside. All of you. Now!"

"Aw Mam" I called back "We want to watch the boar brim our pig."

I didn't see it coming, but I felt something hit me around the ear. You would have thought that I'd have learnt by then - you don't argue with Mam!

So I'd earned myself a sore ear for my trouble and still hadn't found out what brimming was, never mind see the boar brim our pig!

Anyway, a few months later, the sow produced a litter of eight piglets. They were really cute and everyone was excited and kept going to look at them. Now, they may have been really cute and we may have all been excited, but that didn't mean that we all went soft. From the day they were born, we set to work to fatten them up, so that Dad would get a good price for them at the market.

Soon enough the day came that Dad decided that the little fellas were fat enough and it was time for them to take a trip to the market. The decision made, Dad put seven of the piglets into crates and loaded them onto the cart. The eighth little piggy, who I had christened Dolly, we kept – and she were right tasty too!

I'd never seen Mam happier. She loved looking after the animals and the numbers of our stock were starting to grow. We had hens, Mary the cow and now a sow and a litter of little piglets. Things were definitely looking up at Pondhill.

*

Funnily enough, the more things looked up at the farm, the more visits we got from relations, a number of whom I'd never even heard of, never mind knew! Numerous aunts, cousins and the like would come over to farm. Their visits got to be more and more regular, despite the fact that it was a long walk for them. They were always made welcome, and it may well be the fact that they enjoyed our company that kept them coming back with increasing regularity, but I don't think so. Call me cynical, but I think it were more the fact that they got a good feed and went home loaded up with cheese, butter, eggs, cream, some bottled fruit, etc.

I think Dad got a bit fed up with them coming over quite so often, but Mam said we had to look after the family. So it continued and, if any of the aunts and cousins couldn't come to the farm for some reason, mam would take bags full of farm produce to them.

At the time, the black market was thriving, which is understandable when you remember that rationing was in full swing and people were really limited in what they were allowed. Each person was restricted by rationing to the following each week:

12oz sugar;

4oz butter;

meat to the value of 1/10d;

2oz tea;

2oz margarine;

2oz cooking fat

and only 1oz of cheese.

The war affected lots of other things that we all take for granted now. For instance, everyone was also told not to exceed 5 inches of water in their bath – not that that bothered me at the time!

The availability of new clothing was also severely restricted, with everyone being issued clothing coupons. Not only did the brides of the day have to forget any ideas they may have had about fancy wedding dresses, I remember that the use of sugar for cake icing was prohibited and, because of this tiered wedding cakes were frequently made of cardboard!

It wasn't just the lack of nice dresses and wedding cakes that women had to put up with either. Women played a vital role during the war, keeping their families fed and clothed, despite the rationing and so many working in munitions factories to support the needs of the war, or on the land to keep the nation fed. All this done whilst worrying for their husbands, sons, brothers and loved ones who were fighting abroad.

So, like I said, given everything that was going on, it was no surprise that there was a thriving black market. I think Mam might have dealt a bit in the black market, because we always had enough tea and sugar – but they were always kept out of sight in a cupboard.

10
THE END OF THE WAR

Everyone had experienced the hardship of the war, but at long last it was over. 8th May 1945 was V.E. day and family and friends were celebrating. There was plenty of laughing, but also a lot of crying. Tears of joy for the loved ones who had come home and tears of sorrow for the ones that didn't.

There were some major changes straight away - now, people could leave their gas masks at home and didn't have to have them round their neck when they went to work or to school. Some things though didn't change, with food still in short supply and everyone still having ration books.

Mam and Dad were just happy that all of the family were safe. We were fortunate that, throughout the war, we hadn't experienced a serious air raid in the village. In total, the village had lost seven young men to the war. A total that was thankfully low, but each one was a tragedy for the family and friends left behind.

School continued much the same as always, with Mrs Scott still shouting and regularly going into a rage. I swear that the wart on her cheek was getting bigger and it was a regular topic of conversation for Clive and me. We would make each other laugh, imagining it growing and covering her face completely. If she'd known what we were thinking she would have had the rage to beat all rages!!

Suddenly the weeks had gone by and it was December. This would be the first Christmas after the war had ended and all the kids were excitedly talking about Christmas and what they hoped Father Christmas would bring them. I was excited and full of anticipation, but Mam and Dad had made it clear that there wasn't any spare money for luxuries, so I knew I wasn't going to get lots of presents. Dad did tell me that he would have a word with Father Christmas, which made me very happy, because I knew that Dad would tell Santa that I was a good lad.

I was still a bit worried though, in case Santa didn't know where Pondhill was, so I decided to write him a letter. When I told everyone they all told me it was a really good idea and Madge said she would help me to write to him.

Mam was busy working on her tab rug and was determined to have it made in time for Christmas. For all her determination though, having it finished for Christmas wasn't looking likely, as it was taking longer than expected to make. Mam knew exactly what the problem was - she didn't have enough rags. This was hardly a surprise, as after all, we were still wearing the rags! Luckily, our clothes were saved when, a few days later, Ada arrived home from work with a large bag crammed full of old woollen jumpers and bits of satin cloth. Mam was over the moon with her acquisition and straight away began cutting up the clothes into suitably sized strips. Mam worked at pegging the rug night after night, racing against the calendar,

As Christmas drew near, there was another job that needed to be done. We were all sat there eating one night when Mam looked across at Dad and announced, in a matter of fact way, that Dolly should be slaughtered.

The first time I'd gone to feed her, after her siblings had been taken to market, I told her that I'd decided to call her Dolly. Every day, when I fed her, I'd give her a slap and a tickle and talk to her and she would answer me with a mixture of squeals and grunts. Now Dolly the little pig was going to be slaughtered.

Mam carried on talking, pointing out that Dolly was plump, succulent and ready for slaughtering and it would mean that we'd have some nice pork or ham for Christmas.

Whilst I was listening to what she was saying, I felt a bit sick, but, as young as I was, like most kids in those days who lived on farms, I'd always known and accepted that the pig would be slaughtered for Christmas.

Dad made the necessary arrangements and, on the chosen day, Mr Jackson, my friend Maurice's Dad, arrived at Pondhill. He was a tall thin man who didn't say much and always wore a flat cap. The other thing he always did was chew twist, which you might know as chewing tobacco, which meant that he was always spitting.

"Let's get on, bring her out and put her on the wood-chopping block" he said and followed it up by giving a big spit, which flew through the air and landed about a foot from where I was standing. I watched this in awe of the man, wishing that I could spit like that. Whenever I did a spit, it all went down the front of my jumper!

Poor Dolly. Her legs were tied and she was carried, squealing with terror, to the block. I stuck my fingers in my ears to deaden Dolly's cries. Mam saw me and told me to go into the house. She didn't have to tell me twice, I ran as fast as I could, my fingers still in my ears.

Mam followed me in and I watched her pick up a large bowl. "It's to catch the blood, to make black pudding" she told me, as she went back outside with the bowl. It was only when Mam came back into the house and went over to the range that I noticed that a big pot had been filled with boiling water, which Mam was now further topping up.

What's all the hot water for Mam? It isn't bath day."

"It's to get Dolly's bristles off."

Mam could see that I looked confused, so she explained that, because pig bristles are so tough, they either have to be burned off, or softened by pouring boiling water over the skin and then scraped off.

I didn't say anything else as Mam carried the tub of boiling water out of the house. In my head I was picturing Dolly screaming in pain as boiling water was poured over her. It didn't occur to me at the time that she would already be dead before the boiling water was used.

The deed was done. About two hours later, my Dad came in to the kitchen and asked if I wanted the pig's bladder. Now, all farm kids know that a pig's bladder makes a great football when it's blown up. Suddenly all memories of Dolly faded and my sadness turned to joy - I had a football! Monday suddenly seemed a long time away and I couldn't wait for it to arrive, so I could show Clive my prized possession and we could play football in the school playground.

Dad and Mam finished off what had to be done with the pig. The fat was rendered for lard, tasty on bread with a sprinkle of salt. The side of bacon was put on the stone slabs in the back kitchen and salted and the hams were hung from hooks in the kitchen ceiling just above the range, where the smoke would help to keep it until it was cured ready for eating. If any ham was still left when summer came, the smoke from the range would stop bluebottles from striking the ham. This didn't always work and, sometimes, the bluebottles won and you would see a few maggots falling of the ham on to the kitchen floor. When this happened, Dad would get a knife and scrape the surface of the ham, to get rid of the maggots. Hygiene? A few maggots weren't a problem!

Monday came at long last, off to school with my prized possession, my now smelly pig's bladder. Clive was waiting at the school gate.

"What have you got there, Joe?"

My little chest was puffed out, as I proudly replied "It's a pig's bladder."

"A what? I've never seen owt like that before" Clive admitted.

"Well it makes a smashing football. Let's go and play footie in the playground."

No sooner were the words out of my mouth when the school bell interrupted and called us into the class room. I was gutted.

I hid the bladder under my desk, on the floor, but when we stood up for prayers I must have kicked it, because it rolled out from its hiding place, across the classroom floor.

Suddenly, above the noise of scraping chairs came a high pitched shriek from one of the girls. This was soon followed by another, then another, until everyone joined in and the room shook with the deafening sound of their combined screams.

Only Clive and I sat motionless, helplessly watching my prized possession rolling around the classroom floor.

After what seemed an eternity, a hushed silence fell over the classroom. I will never forget the thunderous look of pure rage on Mrs Scott's face. Her eyes were sticking out like golf balls, her face a colourful mix of red and blue. For a second she didn't speak.

Clive whispered, "Flipping heck, Joe."

I didn't answer, my mouth was too dry. The silence was broken when Mrs Scott finally exploded.

"Who brought this into my class room?"

I took a deep breath, stood up and swallowed hard.

"Me," I croaked, "it's a pig's bladder and it makes a good football."

Mrs Scott stormed over to me, grabbed me by my ear and dragged me to where the bladder had come to a halt.

"Pick it up, take it outside and put it in the dustbin, then come back in and I will take you to see the headmaster" she hissed. "How could you bring such a horrid, dirty, foul thing to school and terrify the children."

"It's only a pigs bladder," I muttered, which turned out to be the wrong thing to say. The next thing, I felt the leg of a child's chair hitting me across my shoulder and I fell right next to where the bladder lay waiting.

"PICK IT UP," she bellowed, "and put it in the bin, then it's straight to the headmaster for you!"

Now going to the headmaster is scary, but when I told him how I had got the bladder, about Dad slaughtering my pig, Dolly, so that we would have pork or ham for Christmas dinner, he decided that the punishment I had already received was sufficient.

I genuinely thought that he had sympathy for me, about Dolly being killed. It took me a long time to realise that actually he was hoping for a bit of ham or pork for Christmas. As far as I can remember, I don't think he got any.

11
CHRISTMAS 1945

It had taken forever, but at last Christmas had arrived!

I opened my eyes and began the task of unravelling myself from two huge ex-army coats that covered the bed in place of eiderdowns. Finally succeeding, I scurried to the side of the bed and looked over the edge. My eyes widened as I saw, not one, not two, but three presents! They were lying there, wrapped in newspaper, and they were for me! I was so excited that Santa had not forgotten me.

I shouted out "Santa's been," as I scrambled off the bed. Madge came into the bedroom to help me unwrap my presents, giggling at my excitement. I had a new pullover, well nearly new, and a tipper wagon (which I found out years later, Denis had made at his work). This was the first new toy I had ever had; no other kid had played with it. My third present was an orange.

With my presents unwrapped, I turned to Madge.

"What did Santa bring you, Madge?"

"Oh, some hankies, a pinny and an orange" she told me.

I think Madge was a bit disappointed with what Santa had brought her, but I couldn't wait to pull on my clothes and go and play with my new toy.

I ran downstairs clutching my new prized possession and was greeted by the welcoming glow of blazing wood burning in the cast-iron range, with Mam's new tab rug laid out on the floor in front of it. I remember thinking how cosy the kitchen looked, as Mam, Dad, Denis and Ada sat there smiling and wishing me and Madge a Merry Christmas.

"So what did Santa bring you two?" everyone wanted to know.

"Look at this tipper wagon, it's the best present ever" I said, as I ran round the kitchen floor, pulling it behind me and showing off my new pullover at the same time.

"Now thee lot, you don't go on that rug wi' clogs on hast thee heard me?" Mam announced.

"Aye, we heard thee love" Dad told her, with a big grin on his face.

We all agreed Mam had made a good job of the rug and that it brightened up the kitchen. What none of us realised at the time was that the rug was not going to be a permanent fixture. As soon as Christmas Day was over, it was put away and only brought out on Sundays and when the Aunts and Uncles came to visit!

Mam had already started cooking the leg of pork (poor Dolly) for Christmas dinner.

"Eeh Ada lass that pork smells reet good." Dad said what we were all thinking.

"We'll be hevin a reet good dinner today. No empty bellies, we'll fill up till we're nigh brussen" said Mam, breaking into a smile.

I perhaps should explain that 'nigh brussen' was a good old York-shire expression that you might better understand as 'near bursting'.

About mid-day, Ethel with her husband Leonard and their son Val, along with Aunt Maggie, Uncle Brian and cousins, Harold, Margaret and Doreen, all arrived for Christmas dinner. The kitchen was full of people all wishing everyone a merry Christmas. Aunt Maggie was ad-miring the rug and Dad gave Uncle Brian and Leonard a glass of the elderberry wine that Mam had made.

"By Joe, that's gone reet to the spot. It fair warms thee up." Uncle Brian told Dad contentedly. He looked content too, so much so that Aunt Maggie suddenly piped up.

"You all know that I don't drink, but it is Christmas, so I think I'd like to try it."

The bottle was soon emptied and everyone was laughing and sporting red cheeks, especially Aunt Maggie!!

We all sat down at the kitchen table and Dad carved Dolly's leg. I must admit I did feel a bit guilty about enjoying the smell of the pork, but by gum it did look good!

Mam shared the dinner out; potatoes, cabbage, turnip, apple sauce and bread stuffing. After that we had bottled fruit and cream, with Christmas cake and cheese to finish the dinner. We all left the table bruson. Aunt Maggie and Uncle Brian said it was the best Christmas dinner ever. Aunt Maggie wanted to know how Mam had got dried fruit and sugar to make a fruit cake - Mam said nowt!

All too soon it was time for them to leave. A neighbour with a horse and cart was going to take them back over the moor to Oxenhope. Before they left, Mam filled them each a basket with cheese, ham, eggs and butter.

"Oh Ada, you don't have to do that" Aunt Maggie said, her hand taking the basket even as she started to speak, "but it is good of you."

We all waved them goodbye and watched the horse and cart go off down the lane.

When we were back indoors, Denis piped up, "That was a good Christmas day, but by gum can that lot eat! You would think they had never had 'owt to eat before. And then, on top of it all, our Mam gave them each a basket full of food to tek 'ome!"

Dad didn't say anything, but we all knew that he was a bit annoyed at Mam giving food away again.

Christmas was over, then New Year came and went and everything carried on in 1946 just the same as it had in 1945. Madge and I went back to school, Dad, Denis and Ada were working and Mam was looking after the farm. Polly, our horse, was getting on in years and the land round the farm was hard work for her. Dad said he would have to look out for a good, strong, younger horse this coming spring, even though that would cost money, which, he reminded everyone, was in short supply. He said he'd keep looking anyway, in case something turned up.

12
THE BOGIE

One particular weekend we were going to start collecting, or progging, for what we all called 'plot night', which people probably know better nowadays as bonfire night.

We always started collecting long before the 5th November, because we were always determined that our bonfire would be the biggest in the village. We loved plot night and looked forward to tucking in to Mam's homemade plot toffee, which was widely acknowledged as the best in the village. Just thinking about it now I can still taste it - by gum it was good!

After progging for a while we got a bit fed up and, given that we had plenty of time before plot night to build the bonfire, started looking for something else to do.

Down in the village, we saw one of the village lads playing with a soapbox bogie, which was a popular pastime for young lads back then. Clive and I decided we would set to and build one and raced back to Pondhill as fast as we could.

What we needed was an old pram, so off we went to our usual supplier - the tip. After a good bit of rooting around we found just what we wanted, a set of large pram wheels complete with an unbent axle. Next to them was a smaller pair of wheels, we couldn't believe our luck. Back we hurried to the farm with our bounty, where we found a plank of wood to support both sets of wheels and screwed it onto the axles. Now all we needed was a wooden orange box which we would secure to the plank of wood and we would have our bogie.

"Let's go down to the Greengrocers - he will have an orange box" Clive said, getting all excited. So off we ran, back to the village, as fast has our legs would carry us, hardly slowing as with excited smiles spread across our faces, we charged into the greengrocers. Our smiles were even wider when we emerged a minute later with the crate we had been given.

It was all uphill coming back and it took a lot of effort to carry the orange box back to the farm. As excited as we were, we had to stop and rest a few times on the way.

However, as soon as we got there we set to work. We nailed the box onto the plank of wood and then put a bolt through the plank to the front axle, enabling the bogie to be steered. Finding a length of rope to operate the steering, we fitted it and, finally, our creation was ready.

I elected myself to be the driver and, taking up the steering rope in both hands, plonked myself down at the front of the crate, with my clogs resting at either end of the front axle. Not to be left out, Clive crammed his small frame into the remaining space behind me. Both in position, Clive grasped the rear wheels with both hands and rolled the bogie forward – we were off.

As we started down the steep hill, we soon picked up speed and, whilst we laughed and shouted out encouragement to each other, the bogie raced down the hill like a bat out of hell. We were going faster and faster and loving it, until we suddenly realised that we were fast approaching the village.

If there was a design fault with our bogie it was the brakes. Basically, the braking system consisted of my clog irons. That day, in an attempt to slow down the bogie, which by now was hurtling down the hill at break-neck speed, I forced down both clogs to engage with the road surface. To my horror I discovered that I could not slow down the speeding death trap. From his cramped position behind me Clive, white-faced, was pleading with me to stop the bogie. For both of us, the fun and excitement had quickly turned to sheer terror.

Terrified, and pulling for all I was worth on the steering rope, I desperately kept trying to slow our speed. My clog irons were throwing up great showers of sparks as they skimmed along the road.

"Turn into the rec!" I could just hear the terrified shout from Clive above the noise of my own shrieks.

Looking ahead I could see the local rec, or park, hurtling towards us.

"Hang on!" I yelled back, as I yanked on the rope to turn the front wheels to the left.

The speeding bogie screamed in protest, as it shuddered, bounced and rocked violently from side to side, but somehow stayed intact and the right way up, as it veered left and onto the rec. It bucked, hurdled and lurched over everything in its path, until finally it came to a stop on top of a flower bed.

For what seemed to be eternity, but in reality was probably only a mere few seconds, everything was quiet and totally still. From where he remained jammed in the crate behind me, Clive broke the silence.

"Heck, I thought we were both goners there!"

We both just sat there, shaking from head to foot, our legs feeling like jelly, but thankful that we were both alive.

Reality returned with the booming voice of authority.

"What the hell do you think you two daft buggers were doin' racing down the road on that dammed death trap, frightening folk half to death?"

We looked up to see the large figure of the village bobby looming over us.

I think he must have seen the fear and terror still etched on our ghostly white faces, for he took pity on us.

"You could have killed yourselves, now get off home and don't let me see you down here again in that thing!"

All we could do was to keep saying that we were very sorry. When, finally, he had gone, we both agreed that we had got off lightly – not only had we escaped from our ride of terror without a scratch, when it had seemed certain to us as we had been careering down the hill that death was waiting for us at the bottom, we had even managed to avoid getting a clout round the ear hole from the bobby. Whilst we might have got away with it physically, we didn't feel like celebrating because we were both badly shaken up.

Our legs were still shaking beneath us, as we began the long walk home, pulling the bogie slowly along behind us.

"It can't half travel fast that bogie, we were reet lucky we haven't broken our necks."

As I heard Clive's words, whilst I agreed with him, I also had to share a worrying thought with him.

"Our necks might yet end up broken – I hope that bobby doesn't tell our Mams!"

13
BONFIRE NIGHT

Clive, Norman, Maurice and me started progging again, for our bonfire night. For many families, Guy Fawkes Night became a domestic celebration and there was an unspoken competition to see which Mam could make the best plot toffee and parkin pigs.

Now, for those of you from Yorkshire, no explanation will be needed, but for anyone reading this I'd better explain that parkin pigs are ginger biscuits, baked in the shape of a pig, that traditionally were made for Halloween and bonfire night. I think most people will have heard of plot toffee, although it goes under different names, such as bonfire toffee or treacle toffee. It's a brittle, treacle toffee that again was traditionally made for bonfire night celebrations.

When I was little, every Mam had their own jealously guarded recipe for both plot toffee and parkin pigs and us kids soon learnt not to praise someone else's toffee or biscuits whilst you were in earshot of your own Mam!

My Mam's toffee was always the best - everybody said so, even if they told their own Mam that hers was best. Even now, when I think about it, I can still taste Mam's toffee, by gum, it was reet good.

Anyway, back to the story. All of us lads started collecting wood and owt else we could find which would burn. Norman brought part of a wooden gate.

"I hope tha father won't be angry about thee bringing this" I said to him.

"Nay, he won't be - he doesn't kna" Norman replied.

"If tha father gets to kna tha'd get thee arse kicked" Maurice piped up.

We all burst out laughing, before continuing the serious job of progging.

I remember our next job was making an effigy of Guy Fawkes. He would eventually sit on top of the bonfire, but before that he had a job to do!

We found an old sack for his body and stuffed it with old rags and whatever filling we could find that was suitable.

Maurice's Mam gave us a pair of very old trousers. Now we had a body and legs, but how do you put arms on a sack?

Clive came up with the good idea of getting a piece wood, putting it through the sack, so that you have an arm sticking out of either side of the sack.

Next we needed summat to cover the wood. We decided that a jacket, or old jumper, would be ideal, but folk didn't throw things away back then.

Our Ada came to the rescue. She had told someone at work about what we were doing, but that we needed a jacket for Guy Fawkes. I think the bloke must have been sweet on her, because two days later we had a jacket.

We all agreed that our Guy was looking good, but, to be honest, it was barely recognisable from a bundle of rags and, most importantly, we still needed a head. Mam gave us an old, soft straw shopping bag, which we stuffed with straw and tied onto the sack with string. Maurice was good at drawing and he said he would draw a face on a brown paper bag, which we could then pull over the stuffed shopping bag and our head would be complete.

Come Saturday morning we were all ready to put our plan into action.

I got Dad's wheelbarrow and we put the Guy in it. After standing back and admiring our creation for a few seconds, off we went, down into the village.

We all congregated on the street corner and planted a big sign, saying 'Penny for the Guy', on the front of the wheelbarrow.

We were there ages and I think we got three pennies.

We decided that, if we were going to make a fortune, we'd have to change our plan. Soon it was agreed, we would go from door to door. We took it in turns to knock on the door and say "penny for the Guy missus."

Sometimes, we would be given a penny, but, on a few occasions, the husband came to the door and we got a clout round the earhole and told to bugger off.

At the end of the day we were all cold and hungry, but we had three pennies each which, I'm sad to say, we viewed as a great success!

The night before bonfire night was 'mischief night'. This was the night when rival gangs competed to see who could build the biggest bonfire and, sometimes, a gang would burn the wood collected by their opponents. Every year we would be worried that our bonfire would be attacked, but nobody ever tried to set fire to it. At the time we were convinced that our bonfire was always spared because the other gangs were scared of us. Looking back, I think that we were too far out of the village for them to bother.

Come bonfire night and it was always exciting, waiting for the bonfire to be lit.

It was always a big occasion and it seemed to me that the whole village would come out to our bonfire, including everyone from all of the surrounding farms. Dad would stuff lots of straw and paper into the bottom of the bonfire, and then he would get a piece of rag on the end of a long stick which would have been dipped in paraffin. Our Guy Fawkes would be placed on top of the bonfire and then Dad would light the rag and push it into the paper and straw.

The fire took quickly and, as the flames grew, suddenly you could see everyone, all watching in silence, as the flames and sparks shot up into the sky. Now we could light our fireworks.

Clive and I had some jumping jacks.

"Let's put one behind Mr Jackson" I said, full of the mischief of youth.

So we lit one and just put it on the ground right behind him, then ran away and watched. As it went off, he started to jump away from it, but the more he tried to move away, the more it seemed to follow him.

He was doing a reet good imitation of an Irish jig. We laughed until tears streamed from our eyes. Everyone was letting off fireworks and watching as they danced in the sky. When the fireworks had finished, it was time for plot toffee, parkin pigs and not forgetting the spuds. Cooked on the fire, the spuds were always burnt black on the outside and were best part raw on the inside, but we loved them.

*

By the end of the evening, everybody was freezing cold, feeling sick because of the mix and the amount of food that they'd eaten and were tired and ready for their beds. Despite this, everyone was making their way home with smiles draped across their faces.

I can't remember why, but as I was heading back towards the house I made a detour and went into one of the out-buildings, where we kept the hay for the animals. Whatever it was that I had gone in there for, it certainly wasn't what I found. There was a young woman lying on some of the hay. I didn't see who she was, not because she was hidden from view, but because I couldn't help but stare at our Denis, who was standing next to where she was laying, with all of his clothes off and his willy pointing out in front of him!

I didn't know what was happening, but something told me that I'd be in big trouble if either of them saw me, so, as quietly as I could, I reversed back out of the building, my eyes fixed on Denis, or at least a certain part of him, the whole time.

Once outside, I ran to the house, shouted goodnight to everyone and went straight to bed, where I lay trying to work out what on earth Denis and his friend had been doing, why Denis had taken his clothes off on such a cold night and what had happened to his willy.

A few weeks earlier, while fixing some fencing, Dad had hit his thumb with a hammer and it had swollen to twice its normal size. As I finally drifted off to sleep, I figured that Denis must have been hit by a hammer too.

The next morning, still puzzled by what I'd seen, I went to see Norman. If anyone could explain what had been going on it would be Norman. I told him what I'd seen and he burst out laughing. I told him that it wasn't funny and that our Denis had been hit in the willy by a hammer. This just made him laugh more. Finally, he pulled himself together enough so that he could talk.

"Your Denis hadn't been hit with a hammer!"

"Well, what was going on then?" I again asked.

"How can I put this so that you'll understand?" He asked, but didn't wait for a reply before continuing.

"You remember when your father got Mr Binns to bring his boar over, to brim your sow? Well, the lass was like the sow, Denis was the boar and he was about to brim her!"

With that Norman started laughing again.

Not wanting to appear even more stupid than I already felt, I didn't ask any more questions, choosing instead to join in the laughter, as I imagined our Denis as a boar.

14
A WINTRY START TO 1947

The summer of 1946 had been wet and rather cool, but when November came it was unusually warm. Dad was concerned by this, which I didn't understand, so I asked him why.

"Weather like this in November is nowt good, it's a snow breeder!"

Mam gave him one of her looks. "Tha dunno wat tha's talking abart. 'Tis nowt but an old wives' tale, so don't thee fret theesen abart winter."

Unfortunately for everyone, Dad was right. By early December the weather had changed and it was very cold, with snow lying around Pondhill. However, by Christmas, the snow had more or less cleared, the weather had become somewhat milder and we began to think that that was the end of winter. As later events would prove, not only was winter not over, it had in fact only just begun.

I think it was about the 24th January 1947 that winter showed its hand. Madge and I set off to school as usual that morning. The north wind was blowing off the moor and it was bitter cold, as we walked down the road towards the school gates. "No layking about after school, young Joe," Madge told me. "By the look of them clouds we'll have snow before the day is over."

I agreed that it didn't look good. The clouds were a bluish-black and were hanging threateningly over the top of Ickornshaw moor. They were as stunning as they were ominous and they had an hypnotic effect on everyone, drawing people's eyes back to them time and again, as they whispered their message inside everybody's heads, 'winter is returning with a vengeance.'

Having met up with Norman and Maurice as we were walking

down the road, at the school gate we met Clive. There was only one topic of conversation on everyone's lips - the weather.

As we all continued to look towards Ickornshaw Moor, Norman voiced what we were all thinking.

"Hast tha seen that? I ain't seen 'owt like yonder cloud before, it's like a great balloon hanging over tops of Ickornshaw Moor. It's sinister!"

Before we could even agree, the school bell pierced the air and, continuing to glance back as we went, we filed into the school and to our classrooms.

The clouds continued to build and spread over the whole area and, by mid-afternoon, they delivered on their promise, dropping a massive fall of snow which soon blanketed Cowling.

It was decided that the school should close and all of the kids were urged to go straight home, quickly. All the kids that is, except for me. I was told to clear up the classroom and to put all of the chairs up on top of the desks, so that the caretaker could sweep the classroom floor.

By the time that I got out of the classroom, it was four o'clock and terribly dark. Everyone had already gone, including Madge, Norman and Maurice, so I set off for home on my own, tramping through deep snow as I slowly made my way up the road.

The swirling snow came down so thick and fast it was blinding me. The wind blew hard, causing the snow to drift up against the dry stone walls on either side of the lane. It was so deep it was over my clog tops, causing my feet, clad only in thin woollen socks, to feel like blocks of ice. I felt alone and terrified. By now the wind was blowing the snow into gigantic drifts and I feared that I might slip, become buried in a snow drift and nobody would ever find me.

I trudged on, forcing my way through thick snow drifts. My face and hands felt completely numb and I was hunched over, face down, in an attempt to protect my eyes from the icy blast as I placed one step after the other. I was becoming more and more anxious and all I wanted was to see my Mam and home.

Every few steps I'd raise my head slightly and glance ahead, hoping against hope that I'd see Mam. Suddenly, I made out the figure of a tall man a few feet in front of me, walking up the hill. I was not alone!

He was hunched over, treading warily, his head down. I started to walk faster, gaining ground on the man walking ahead. Quickening my pace, slipping and sliding all over the snowy surface, I managed to catch him up. As I reached his side it dawned on me that the man was Mr Jackson, Maurice's dad.

Above the howl of the wind, I shouted to him, desperate to be heard.

"It's me, young Joe from Pondhill, Mr Jackson."

"What the hell are thee doing art in this weather? Get behind me, I'll shield t'snow off thee!" he said.

Mr Jackson was chewing his usual twist and he suddenly spat out a big gob of it, which the wind blew back, so that the wad of spit struck straight in my left eye. My eyes were already sore from the wind and snow, but now it felt like my left one was on fire! I scrabbled around inside my pocket with my frozen hand until I could get my fingers to grip onto a piece of rag, which I quickly pulled out and used to wipe my smarting eye. Fortunately, the rag cleared my eye of the offensive spit, but the burning sensation, whilst not quite as bad, stayed as a memento. Normally I wouldn't have been best pleased about the spit, but at that moment I didn't care, I was just glad to be walking with him.

*

Arriving at the gate of Court House Farm, Mr Jackson said "I'm home now, wilt ye be alreet on your own walking up to Pondhill?"

"Aye, I'll be fine. Goodnight" I bravely replied.

I set off again, once more on my own, battling on through the snow drifts. With my head down, half frozen and getting colder by the minute and with my eye still stinging, I pushed on. My coat and trousers were wet through with the falling snow. I was colder than I'd ever thought possible and was shivering violently. The noise of my teeth chattering was in competition with the howling of the wind and I started to cry.

I remember thinking that I couldn't go any further. I just wanted to give up and sit down in the snow. Right at that moment, when I knew that I couldn't go on, suddenly, I saw the light from a storm lamp ahead. I then heard the most welcoming sound in the world, my Mam's voice, calling to me as she came into sight. She gathered me up into her arms, held me close and I knew that I was safe.

"Let's get you home, lad." Mam smiled at me, then she grasped my hand tight and we trudged the last few yards down the lane to Pond-hill.

Mam soon had me out of my wet clothes and wrapped in a blanket in front of a roaring fire, with a plate of hot meat stew. Everyone was home safe and I wasn't the only one who had done battle with the weather, as Dad had somehow endured a treacherous eight mile walk over the moors from Keighley, because all the buses from Keighley to Cowling had been cancelled due to the roads being blocked by the snow.

What nobody still appreciated at that moment in time, was just how extreme the winter of 1947 was going to be.

15
Winter 1947 Bites Hard

Having thawed out through a combination of the heat from the fire and, not so much eating, as devouring my meat stew, I went straight up to bed. I was so exhausted from my ordeal that I barely managed to undress and have a pee, before crawling into bed, where I instantly fell asleep.

The next morning, I scrabbled out from under the Army greatcoats on my bed and got out of bed. Part of me registered how cold it was, but there was something much more important on my mind, to have a pee! Leaning down, I quickly reached under the bed for the jerry. Before the war, everyone had called them chamber pots, but now, jerry, the slang word for a German soldier, was how most people referred to them. Grabbing hold of the jerry, I brought it out into the open, stood quickly back up and hurried to get into position before my bladder burst!

As I took aim, I looked down and saw that my pee from the night before was frozen in the jerry. Whilst I stood there, doing my best to melt the frozen pee in the jerry, the reality of how cold it was in my bedroom hit me. Looking around, I saw that the windows were covered in a thick layer of ice – on the inside! I finished my pee and made my way over to the window. I tried to look outside, to see what the snow was like, but the ice on the inside of the glass made it impossible to see anything through it. It would have to be scraped away before it would offer up any type of view.

My growing awareness of just how cold it was was accompanied by my body shivering and my teeth starting to chatter. I knew that the fire would be burning red hot in the grate downstairs, so, with some urgency, I grabbed my clothes and ran downstairs. It was too cold to hang about in the bedroom, when I could get dressed by the fire, the only thing that provided heat in the farmhouse.

As I scrambled into my clothes I told mam that my pee was frozen in the jerry, thinking that she'd be as amazed by this as I was. Her response wasn't quite what I'd expected.

"Ay, well's frozen too. When thee's had tha' breakfast wi' thee go and break ice ont it?" The well was our only source of drinking water, so, straight after breakfast, I grabbed an axe and set about the thick ice covering the well.

Each day that the wintry weather continued would see me wielding my axe in delight, smashing through the thick layers of ice on the well, and then helping Dad to fill buckets up with water, which he would then carry into the kitchen, before the water froze over again.

The bitterly cold weather continued, with the severe, freezing conditions showing no sign of easing even after several weeks. The school had been closed since that January day, which was okay by me, but, as the cruel winter dragged on, with deep snow covering the fields, our attempts to get our livelihood, however meagre, from the farm, was becoming increasingly difficult. Food and money were again in short supply. Dad and Denis had managed to get snow clearing work with the council. It was cold, hard work, with poor pay, but as Dad said, it was a bit of money coming into the house.

Coal was hard to come by and had become more costly. To keep the family warm, as well as to use for cooking, Dad had just about chopped up every piece of wood lying around the farm. Any dead or fallen trees were quickly cut up with an axe, or hand saw and hurriedly brought back to the farm. They had to be chopped up and brought to one of the farm's outbuildings on the day that they fell, because if you left them out overnight they would be gone by morning, as everyone was desperately looking for fuel.

Mam's store cupboard was emptying fast and not being replaced.

The hens had stopped laying and every day, when I went in to feed them, I would find another dead hen. They would just be lying there, frozen stiff due to the severe cold. I'd pick the dead bird up and take it to show Mam, who would comment in her typical, down to earth way. "The poor beggar. Oh well, it won't be wasted, for it'll mek us a reet tasty chicken stew. We can't waste good food."

Every time I found a dead hen, we had a lovely chicken stew, but I knew Mam was sad that her hens were dying.

The terrible winter weather continued on day after day. All of the lanes and tracks, despite being dug out by the farmers and the council, were quickly filled in by the wind blowing the snow from place to place. A number of elderly people, living on outlying farms that were hard to reach, died due to the cold. Their coffins were put on sledges and hauled across the snow covered fields to the Black Bull pub, whose cellar became a temporary resting place until the ground thawed out enough to allow the bodies to be buried.

It was impossible to walk down either Treacle Lane, or Old Lane, as the hard frozen snow that covered the lanes was so deep. Because of this, when I went to meet Maurice and Norman, we would have to walk on top of the dry stone walls, before jumping off the wall into the snow, where we would have snowball fights.

The lanes were regularly dug out by council men and we would often stop and watch them digging. On one particular day, though, we saw men working with the council men. They were all wearing the same, strange looking clothes and they had a Police Constable with them!

Norman, who was older than Maurice and me, and who always knew things, told us that they were POW's.

"What's a POW Norman?" we asked.

"German soldier prisoners of war" Norman informed us.

Even though the war was over, many of the German soldiers who had been captured and held in camps across Britain were kept as prisoners, as a form of 'reparation'. They were effectively used as forced labour and it was a full three years after the war had ended before they were all given their freedom.

When Norman told us who they were we were flabbergasted. With eyes wide and jaws dropping, together Maurice and I just said "Blooming 'eck!"

Norman continued, in a voice of authority, enjoying having a captive audience hanging on his every word.

"I've been telled by me father that the men are Germans, enemies of Britain and to keep out of their way. Me father called them Jerries."

Despite having heard the warning passed down by Norman's dad, being young lads and being naturally curious about these foreigners, we would regularly make our way to where they were shovelling snow and peep at them over the wall. Sometimes, some would give us a friendly wave. At first, whenever they did this, we would run away, but, after a while, when they waved we would wave back.

Desperate to share my exciting secret with someone, I told Madge, but she just told me to keep out of their way and not to talk to them.

"I can't talk to 'em", I innocently told her, "I don't understand what they say, they just jabber on to each other!"

"Aye well, but think on and don't go near them Jerries!" Madge, like Norman's dad warned us to keep away.

Naturally, we took no notice of this new warning and continued to fight our way through the snow every day, to wherever they were digging. A few of the Germans could speak broken English and soon they started shouting 'hello' when they saw us. We, in turn, got braver and went from peeping over the wall, to openly standing on the wall to watch them. Soon, we were shouting our own hellos back at them.

As our contact with them grew, so did our conversation. Many of them were very friendly towards us, in particular, one man, who told me that his name was Klaus. He was very tall and had blonde hair and bright blue eyes. I liked Klaus and, as the days and weeks passed, he became my friend. Klaus attempted to teach me a few German words, but I said "Nay Klaus, it teks me all me time at school to learn English!"

Klaus persevered and I did pick up a few German words.

One tea time, Dad had come home early from moving snow. He looked tired. He had managed to buy a bag of coal, but he had had to carry it, on his shoulders, from the village, in deep snow. Mam was fussing over him and made him sit by the fire and have a sup of tea, while she made supper.

Later, as we were sitting around the kitchen table, the whole family quietly having supper, I broke the silence by coming out with a lengthy German sentence.

"Ich bin ein guter Junge."

Before I could say anything else, My Dad exploded with rage. I had never heard or seen him in such a rage and I just looked at him in horror.

"Don't you ever venture again into Pondhill farmhouse speaking like the Jerries, or I will give you a bloody good clout round thy ear!" He bellowed at me.

All I could do was sit there and mutter that I was sorry.

After a while, Madge whispered to me, "What did you say?"

"I said 'I'm a very good boy'" I quietly told her.

"I don't think Dad thought that," she said, laughing.

Life at Pondhill was pretty grim, with the winter seemingly never ending. One late afternoon, just before it got dark, I went out to feed the pig and the few hens that we had left. While I did that, Mam went to milk Mary, the cow. I remember coming back into the house and seeing Madge stoking up the kitchen range.

"By gum, it's cold outside and it's starting to snow again. We 'ater keep house warm," I said and she agreed. Madge went back to her sewing and I filled the iron kettle and put it on the range.

It was half an hour later that we realised Mam hadn't come back into the house after milking the cow. I was reet worried that summat were wrong.

"Let's go and see where she can be," I said to Madge, as I pulled on my coat.

Clutching a storm lamp, we went outside into the pitch dark night. The snow was again coming down fast and, with the wind blowing around us, we walked over to the cow shed. Mary had been milked and was contentedly munching a pile of hay. I looked down and noticed that her water bowls were empty, which was unusual. Mam may have gone over to the well to fill the water bucket.

I was becoming increasingly worried as to where Mam had got to. She was always about the farm and didn't venture far, especially during the current conditions. We left the cow shed and started to shout for her, "Mam, Mam."

Slipping and sliding, we carefully made our way across the surface of the frozen yard, to the well. The well was frozen solid, so she had not got any water from there.

We shouted again. "Mam, where are you?"

I held the storm lamp high above my head, its light reflecting on the frost covered snow. There was no reply.

What we did see, was a large number of Mam's footprints in the snow, but where was she?

It was pitch black, a moonless sky.

"Mam, Mam, where are you?" By now, both of us were crying.

Listening carefully, whilst panning the storm lamp all around, we then heard a muffled cry. It came from the direction of Tinkler beck, at the north side of the farmhouse. Regardless of the icy conditions, we both raced to the edge of the beck.

Then we saw mam and I shouted to her, with tears running down my cheeks, as we hurried to her. When we reached her, she was lying on her back in the snow, both her legs, up to her knees in freezing water, in the ice-covered beck. She was shivering violently and was groaning.

"Madge, grab her left arm and I'll grab t'other. We have to pull her out of the water!" I shouted.

Our Mam was a heavily built woman and therefore extremely heavy. We were both young children, but, nevertheless, with considerable effort we pulled and hauled for what appeared to be an eternity, until we finally managed to pull her out of the beck and up the steep, snow covered, bank. Mam was making a strange, groaning sound, so, without pausing, we continued to half drag and half carry her back to the farm house.

Madge got Mam's wet clothes off and wrapped her in a blanket. Mam was deathly cold and couldn't talk. Her teeth were chattering and both of her legs and ankles were cut and bleeding, as a result of falling through the ice.

We got Mam sat in the armchair, in front of a blazing fire and I mashed a pot of tea. After drinking the hot tea, a little colour started to return to her face.

We placed a bowl of heated water in front of her and lifted her feet into it. Then, we gently bathed the cuts to her ankles and legs.

Being the hard-working woman that she was, Mam quickly started to recover from her ordeal and, seeing our pale, scared faces, told us not to worry

"I'm awreet now. What a daft clot I am. Fancy me falling in t'beck. I was trying to get some water for Mary" she told us, trying to smile, to show us that she was alright.

When Dad came home, at about seven o'clock, he too looked haggard and cold. For over twelve hours he had been snow clearing in horrendous weather conditions. He was extremely concerned on seeing Mam looking so ill and examined the cuts and bruises on her legs.

"From now on, Ada lass, leave the feeding of the stock to me, I'll do it when I get home from work. Young Joe here can fill the buckets of water for the animals and the kitchen."

"Don't thee fret, I'm alreet" Mam said, but we insisted she sat in front of the fire and Madge would make supper.

By late February, the snow started to ease off and the school re-opened. For once I was glad to get back to school and meet up with Clive. We had not seen each other for weeks, as he had been snowed in up Cowling Hill. I had so much to tell him, especially about the Germans and Mam.

16
BUCKING BRONCOS

We lads were always looking for new adventures and didn't need to be asked twice when an opportunity was presented to us. One day, I remember sitting on the wall at Pondhill, looking across the Dean Field land which was next to ours. While I was watching the young heifers in the field, Norman crept up on me.

"What are you up to, young Joe?"

"Nowt much," I told him, "I'm just watching the young stirks that belong to your Dad."

As I looked down from the top of the wall, I noticed that, once again, Norman had some cow muck on his glasses. As usual, I didn't tell him, for it seemed that every time I saw him he would be plastered in either cow muck, or chicken muck.

"Do you fancy having a laik in t'beck?" I asked him,

"Nay young Joe, that's boring stuff," he replied, before adding, "I know – we'll ride me Dad's heifers!"

Norman was on a roll now and, before I could say anything, he continued, excitedly.

"Let's pretend we're bucking broncos, like in Roy Rogers' films!"

"Heck, we'd better not. Your father would kill us if he caught us." I replied nervously,

"Me father's not in, he's gone to market, so we'll be awreet" Norman announced, smiling.

Without further ado, I jumped off the wall and we both ran, laughing, into the field. Pointing to a black and white stirk, which was laid down, chewing its cud, Norman shouted over to me.

"Thee jump on yon beast and I'll jump on this one over here."

Cautiously, coming up behind the cud-chewing stirk, I leapt onto his broad back. As quick as a flash, it rose to its feet and set off, with me holding on for dear life as we raced round the meadow at break neck speed. Both stirks were clearly petrified, but Norman and me were lost in our own make believe world of bronco busting.

Suddenly, above our howls of laughter and the stirks' howls of indignation, we heard a loud, deep voice.

"You two daft buggers! Gerroff me stirks and come aht a that field reet now!"

"Oh Lord, it's me father and he'll give me a reet thrashing" Norman said, with terror in his voice. "But Norman," I said, sharing his terror, "I thought you said he'd gone to market."

"I thought he had. He'll kill me."

My heart was beating so fast and so loud that I could only just hear Norman's reply.

Having jumped off the stirks, with heads bowed down we walked up the field, to where a furious Mr Binns was waiting. I could see how terrified Norman was, so I thought I'd whisper some reassurance.

"If we tell him how sorry we are, he might not kill you."

Norman didn't look reassured.

As soon as we reached Mr Binns, he looked at me and just said "Get back home to Pondhill."

We hadn't had time to even start to say sorry, but I didn't need telling twice to go home. I scurried back to the wall, which was the border of Pondhill and Dean Field. As I climbed the wall, I nervously looked back across the fields, just in time to see Mr Binns' clogged foot coming into contact with Norman's backside.

I walked home, knowing that I wouldn't dare to venture over to Dean Farm to see Norman for several days, until I was sure that the dust had settled. Whilst I was disappointed at the thought of not seeing my mate for a few days, I was relieved that I'd got away without being punished and, by the time I reached Pondhill, my breathing was about back to normal.

I heard a loud slap and felt a stinging sensation in my ear and across the back of my head as soon as I entered the farmhouse. I looked up to see Mam's hand as it started its return journey, having delivered me a good clout round the head. I hadn't got away with it after all.

Nothing much stayed secret at Pondhill. It turned out that Ada had seen Norman and me playing cowboys with the stirks and hadn't wasted any time in running home to tell Mam!

"What on earth were you playing at, riding round the field on t'stirks? What if one had fallen and broken a leg?" Mam was furious.

"I'm reet sorry Mam," I said, "I didn't think."

"Get up to bed, now, and stay there!"

Being sent to bed in the middle of a Saturday was awful, but I knew better than to argue with Mam, so off I went, dragging my feet.

About half an hour later, Clive and Maurice came round to see me. I could hear Mam telling them that she'd sent me to bed and why. After repeating to them how stupid and dangerous what I'd done was, she sent them on their way and shut the door. Out of sight, Clive and Maurice decided not to go home, but instead to come round to the back of the house and call out to me. We started talking through the window, but after a few minutes I got a bit fed up and said I would climb out of the window, scramble onto the lean-to, and then jump down into the garden. Clive and Maurice didn't think much of my idea.

"Nay Joe, tha'll break tha neck and tha's in trouble as it is, without breaking tha neck. Plus, even if you do somehow survive, if your Mam catches you then she may well break your neck anyway!"

"Mams going to Keighley," I told them, "so stop fretting."

With that, I jumped down and took great pleasure in them seeing that I hadn't broken my neck. I was so glad to be out, and to have got out in one piece, that I hadn't given a thought as to how I was going to get back in later on!

Running down the field, quietly and quickly, so as not to be seen by anyone at the farm, we soon arrived at Tinkle Beck. We decided that we each needed a ship and started searching for suitable crafts. Having found a piece of wood each, we were ready to see whose ship would sail the greatest distance down the beck. We approached the side of the beck and proceeded to launch our vessels. All of a sudden, Maurice's foot slipped on the bank and ended up in the beck with the water over his clog, soaking his sock.

Through our laughter, Clive told him to take it off and bang it against a rock, which would soon dry it. Maurice soon had his sock off, but then got a bit carried away. He was jumping up and down and banging the sock on the rock and singing! Clive and I couldn't help but laugh at the sight in front of us, but, after a short while, Clive felt it necessary to stop Maurice's frenzied performance.

"Steady on, Maurice, tha's not going to have any sock left."

Maurice stopped banging the sock and looked at it, to see that, not only was it still soaking wet, but a big hole had also appeared in it!

"What am I going to do? When I get home I'll get a chewed arse!" Maurice cried out.

It was about then that I realised that I, somehow, had to get back upstairs without anyone at home seeing me. So we were quite a quiet three as we made our way back up the field, pondering over what fate awaited us. I asked if anyone had any ideas as to how I could get back upstairs, as I could expect a right clout if I was caught. Maurice said that that was nothing - he wouldn't be able to sit down for a day or two! Clive, well he said that he would be off home; he didn't want to hang around and share in our suffering! I left Clive and Maurice at the garden gate, Clive going as fast as his legs would carry him, Maurice hanging back from going home, knowing what fate awaited him.

As I walked towards the farmhouse door, I was praying that Mam was still in Keighley. I'm sure that my legs were moving slower with every step towards the farmhouse that I took. Finally, I reached the door and could no longer put off opening it to discover my fate. I opened the door and stepped forward, waiting for the clout across the head that would just be the start of what I could expect. It never came.

It only took me a few moments to realise that luck really was on my side that day, because nobody was home. I ran upstairs, went into my room, shut the door and sat on the bed - which is exactly where Mam found me, when she got home and came upstairs to tell me that I could come out of the bedroom now!

17
GOODBYE POLLY, HELLO TOMMY

In the spring of 1947 Dad knew that the time had come when he'd have to replace Polly, our faithful old horse. The severe winter that we had just endured had been one harsh winter too many for her. The old girl was lame and Dad explained to us that this lameness was due to the fact that she was suffering from rheumatism in her joints. I was upset at the thought of Polly leaving the farm, but Dad told me that she would go to a nice place and she wouldn't have to do any more work, which made me feel a lot better.

A week later, a wagon came to take Polly away. I gave her a hug and told her that she was going to a nice place, where she wouldn't have to work. Then, she was put into the wagon and off it drove. I kept waving goodbye to her until the wagon was out of sight.

A few days later, Dad said he'd heard about an eight year old dark bay gelding for sale over at Oakworth. He and Big Norman were going to go in Big Norman's horse and cart and have a look at it, he announced. Dad looked at me and asked if I wanted to go with them – too right I did! As the three of us set off for Oakworth, Dad told me that, if he bought the horse, I could ride it back. I could hardly wait and, as Big Norman kept the horse going at a steady walk, I struggled to stop myself shouting at him to make the mare run, or at least trot! As excited as I was, I knew that I'd get a clout round the 'ead and wouldn't get to ride the horse if I did say 'owt, so, somehow, I kept my mouth shut.

When at last we arrived at the farm, I scrambled out of the cart, ready to go and look at the horse. The farm and farm building looked a bit run down and, as he came over to us, I noticed that even the farmer looked a bit scruffy. The farmer took us over to a shed and told us the horse was inside and we could go in and see it. I looked in through the shed door – it was really dark inside and suddenly I wasn't quite as keen to see the horse.

Following the farmer's invite to go in and see the horse, Big Norman just stood stock still and looked sternly at him. "Bring him outside, we aren't gonna buy t'horse in t'dark!" Norman told the farmer, in a tone that let him know that the topic wasn't up for debate.

The farmer scowled and muttered a bit, but did what Norman asked and proceeded to bring out the horse. Big Norman and Dad started to inspect the animal, running hands all over its back, lifting its feet up and checking each one, then looking in its mouth. After they'd checked it over, Big Norman said something to Dad, and then turned his gaze once again onto the farmer.

"Tha telled us this horse was eight years old. It's nowt a t'sort! 'Appen it's a darn sight neara twelve!"

He didn't take his eyes off the farmer, letting him squirm under his gaze for a few seconds, before he continued. "It'll do job, but thou 'av to bring price down!"

"Nay, I can't do that," the farmer said, but after a short stand-off, he offered a small price drop. That started the bartering. I stood rooted, listening in awe to the arguing and haggling that followed. All of a sudden, it was over and a deal was struck.

"Tha's getten a good horse. It's strong in t'back and it's getten a good neck. There's plenty 'a work in this horse." Big Norman whispered to Dad after the deal was done.

So, after a spit on the hand, followed by a handshake, money was exchanged. Then, Big Norman said to the farmer, "Art thou goner give us a bit luck then?"

"Nay," came the reply, "tha knaws tha's getten a good deal wi'horse!"

Again Big Norman fixed him with a look and, scowling again, the farmer reached into his pocket, then gave Dad half a crown.

So, after a leg up on to the horse, I trotted on home behind the horse and cart, Dad regularly looking back to check that I hadn't fallen off. It wasn't until I was sitting on that horse's back and looking down, seeing how high above the road I was, that I realised how big a horse of 15/16 hands actually was.

We arrived at the top of Treacle Lane, after the eight mile trek over the moors from Oakworth, thankful it had been a fine day. Dad scrambled out of the cart, thanking Big Norman for his help. "Think nowt abart it," replied Big Norman, before shouting to his horse, "trot on, my bonnie," as he made his way back to his farm.

Dad took the reins, leading the horse the last few yards to Pondhill. Mam, Denis and Ada were all waiting in the farm yard to see the arrival of the new horse. After a lot of looking over the horse and talking about it and the deal, everyone agreed we now had a fine horse. Then Dad announced that, because I had done so well riding it home, I could take it down to the blacksmith's in Ickornshaw, for shoeing, on Monday morning, on the way to school.

I was so excited that I had to go and tell someone. Norman! He would be at home. So, off I went at full speed to find him. When I got to his farm, I found him in the pig hole, mucking the pigs out and, as usual, he had pig muck on his glasses.

"Norman what do you think, we have got a new horse and Dad said I can ride it down to the blacksmith Monday on the way to school."

I rattled it out, not even pausing for breath, I was that happy. That was when Norman dropped the bomb shell.

"Aye, me Father said you'd getten a new horse, 'cos other one went to knacker's yard."

I didn't want to hear it, let alone believe it.

"No, no, she didn't," I stammered, "Polly's gone to a nice home, where she doesn't have to work anymore!"

Norman insisted that it had gone to the knackers yard, and, even as he said the words, something inside me told me it was true.

I ran home, my legs only running marginally faster than the tears that were racing down my cheeks. All the way home the same question repeated itself over and over again in my head. How could Dad send Polly to the Knackers yard?

I ran straight into the kitchen, tears still streaming down my face, to find both Mam and Dad sitting there.

"What on earth is the matter with you, young Joe?" Dad asked.

"You told me Polly had gone to a good home, but you sent her to the knackers yard!" I half shouted and half sobbed.

Dad looked at me and then spoke, in as sympathetic a voice as I'd ever heard from him.

"Yes, I had to send her to knackers yard. She was in a lot of pain with her rheumatism and, sometimes in life young Joe, you have to make a decision which you might not want to, but it's what's best for the animal. I'm sorry I didn't tell you Joe, but we knew you would be upset. There was nowt we could do for Polly, lad. The kindest thing was to have her put down."

I didn't say anything, because, as young as I was, something inside me told me that Dad was right, but I was still upset at the thought that Polly had gone to the knackers yard. I ran out of the kitchen and went to one of my favourite places, the Cuckoo Rock. From the Cuckoo Rock you could see down the valley to the edge of the village, even the church clock tower. On top of that, you could also see all round the moor. I would sit there and listen to the grouse and the birds on the moor. It was quiet and peaceful; at least it was until the 12th of August, when the Grouse season started.

We always knew when it was the 12th of August. From all directions, the toffs would arrive, then head onto the moor and start shooting the Grouse.

They talked so posh that none of us had a clue what they were talking about! They acted as if they owned the moor and wasted no time in summoning the police whenever one of the local cloth cap men dared to go out shooting Grouse. Despite knowing what would happen, the locals took great delight in going out shooting and upsetting the toffs. The police would duly arrive, but they never did catch anyone.

After sitting at Cuckoo Rock for a while, hunger took over, so I walked back to the farm, where I knew Mam would have something nice cooking on the range. I opened the door and, as expected, Mam was stood by the range watching over something boiling in a cast iron pan. Mam was watching me as I stood by the door.

"That smells good, Mam." I interrupted the silence.

"Yes love, it's a rabbit stew." She replied. Her face full of sympathy, she went on, "Ater alreet? Ye haven't to fret theesel over Polly."

"Aye, Mam. I know it was best for Polly. I'm alreet now."

Monday morning arrived and, before Dad left for work, he brought Tommy - that was our name for the new horse, out of the field and into the stable. He left instruction with Mam that I had to put the bridle on Tommy and take him straight down to the blacksmiths on the way down to school. "Tell him, no laikin about on the way!"

I ate my breakfast so fast that I nearly choked. Mam told me to slow down, but I was too excited to do that. As I was shovelling my breakfast down, I wondered what Clive would say when he saw me riding on Tommy.

I ran out of the kitchen and sprinted across to the stable, where I stopped dead in my tracks and gulped. Tommy looked twice the size stood in the stable than he had outside.

"Blooming heck," I said out loud. I looked at the size of him and realised that I wouldn't even be able to reach up to his head to put on his bridle. Panic began to set in, but then, as with so many other times in my life when I didn't know what to do, all of a sudden, from behind me, came a voice that always meant that everything was going to be alright.

"Here, let me do that," Mam gently said, as she took the bridle off me and, effortlessly, put it on Tommy.

"Come here, Joe, and I'll give you a leg up," she smiled at me.

As we came out of the stable, Mam gave me an encouraging look.

"Wilt tha be alreet?"

I heard a small croak, that sounded like it came from somewhere far away,

"Aye," it said, and I realised that it had come from my mouth.

So, nervously, I set off, sitting high above the farm yard as Tommy and I walked slowly through the gate and out onto Treacle Lane.

I talked non-stop to Tommy all the way along Treacle Lane, feeling more comfortable with every step that my new friend took. By the time we got to Old Lane, I'd forgotten why I had ever been nervous and felt like Roy Rogers!

I met Maurice and Norman on the way down to school and, with a smile as wide as my face, gave them a wave. Both of them agreed that Tommy was a grand horse and both wanted a ride, but I said no, I had to get it to the blacksmiths before school. To be truthful, if I had got off I would not have been able to get back on, and I was not going to give Maurice and Norman the pleasure of seeing me struggling to get back on Tommy! Nothing was going to stop me from arriving at the school on horseback!

When I neared the school, Clive was at the school gate and he came running towards me.

"What ye doing?" he shouted.

"Going to blacksmiths - do you want to get up behind me?"

"Oh, yeah!" He excitedly replied, "But how do I get onto the horse?"

"Come over and climb on to farmers milk kit stand, then put your right leg over horse's back and hang onto me while you slide over," I suggested, suddenly being an expert in how to mount Tommy.

After a bit of a struggle, Clive got up behind me. All the kids came over, wanting a ride, but by now I was showing off. I just clipped my heels into Tommy's flanks and we were off at a trot.

"Steady on, Joe," Clive shouted out, as I nearly fell off, but, although I was clinging on for dear life, I wasn't going to admit to any nerves.

"Just hang on to me, you'll be alreet!" I shouted confidently back.

Somehow, we made it to the blacksmith's without Clive falling off. I pulled on the reins and Tommy came to a stop. Clive looked down and I felt his grip on me get even stronger.

"Flipping 'eck, Joe, it's a long way down. How are we gonna get off?"

The forge open frontage, leading into the dark, smoke-blackened interior, faced out onto Ickornshaw Road. Fastened to one wall was an iron rail, used for tethering horses that were waiting to be shoed. There was a huge iron anvil, where the blacksmith would hammer a bar of white hot iron into shape, to make shoes for the horse. There was also a big set of bellows, for keeping the furnace hot and you'd often see kids standing outside, watching, fascinated by the blacksmith working at his anvil, marvelling at the sparks flying, whilst he hammered a bar of white hot iron.

Jod, the blacksmith, was a huge man, with well-muscled arms, a broad chest and shoulders. He was known to everyone and was well respected for his work. He walked over towards us.

"Now, young Joe, what have we here?" he asked, as he wiped the sweat from his brow with a piece of rag.

"Shoeing all round please, Jod." I confidently chirped.

"Well, you'll ater get off horse, or have I to shoe him with you two sat on his back?"

My confidence suddenly drained, as I realised I would have to admit that we couldn't get down. I opened my mouth, ready to make our embarrassing admission, but, before I could say anything, two strong arms came up, reached around us both, and we were suddenly standing on the road.

"Tell thee father he'll be ready at dinner time," Jod told us and, with a wave, we set off back to school.

When we got to the school gate, all the kids came clambering around Clive and me, especially the girls. They were all asking about Tommy and we happily told them tales of how fast we could gallop on him.

"I think you should ride Tommy down to school every day if the girls are going to hang around us like this!" Clive whispered to me and I could feel myself blushing, which just made Clive laugh.

"Oh, Joe, you're doing an imitation of a tomato again."

Before I could even attempt to reply, the bell rang out and we all had to file into the classroom.

The morning seemed to go on forever. All I could think about was Tommy and riding him back to Pondhill, but I was brought back to earth by a ringing in my ear, as Mrs Scott's loud voice told me to listen and pay attention. At last, the bell rang, announcing that it was dinner time. Clive and I both rushed into the dining hall, sliding to a halt as we reached the counter where the dinner ladies were serving.

"My, you two are in a rush for your dinner" one of them said.

She looked on, shaking her head as we grabbed our plates, found our seats and started devouring our dinner as though we hadn't eaten for a week. I finished first and implored Clive to eat quicker. "I can't guzzle my dinner like you can, Joe, it would make me sick."

That might have been what he said, but, as I turned to leave, Clive jumped up to follow me out of the dinner hall, after all he didn't want to miss out on riding Tommy.

We ran all the way back to the blacksmith's forge. Tommy was stood outside, all newly shod.

"Are ye riding him back to Pondhill now?" Jod asked.

"No, just to the school, then I'll ride home after school." I breathlessly told him.

"Well see you tether him up safe and secure. You don't want him running off." Jod advised us, as he gave Clive and me a leg up onto Tommy.

With that, we waved a goodbye and, sat high above the world once more, off we went.

Clive said that we were like cowboys in the pictures and, laughing, we pretended to be our cowboy heroes all the way back to school.

When we arrived at the school, all the lasses came running up to look at Tommy. Clive nudged me, "We 'aven't had lasses running around us like this before," he said, grinning like the cat that got the cream.

For once, I wasn't interested in the girls' attention. All I wanted to do was to find a secure place to tether Tommy in the playground, where I could see him from the classroom.

I tied him to the school railings and told all the kids to keep away from him. With Tommy securely tethered, I went into the classroom. I hadn't even had time to sit at my desk, when I heard the very familiar sound of Mrs Scott shouting.

"Have you no common-sense Joe Sawley! What in heaven's name made you think that you could bring a horse to school?"

"It's been at the blacksmith's and I'm taking it home after school," I told her.

"Oh, no you are not! You are taking it home right now!"

Her shouting echoed around the classroom.

I could not believe my ears, Mrs Scott letting me leave the class-room to take Tommy home. I reached the door in two strides, thinking that I had got the rest of the day off, but her shrill voice followed me, telling me in no uncertain tones to get back to school as soon as I'd taken Tommy home, without delay.

I went over to Tommy, who was standing quietly, still tethered to the railing and took him across to the farmers milk kit stand. It was easy to mount him from there, because the stand came up to Tommy's belly. My legs over his back, I clipped his flanks with my heels and we were away, Tommy's shoes clattering on the road and me, sat proudly, and hoping that the kids in the classroom could see us trotting along the road. We trotted until the school was out of site, then I just let him plod on. It was all uphill going home and I didn't want to tire him out, after all, I was in no hurry to get back to school. With that in mind, I even let him stop a few time for a rest!

Mam was surprised to see me home early and, I think relieved to know everything had gone to plan. She said that Jod had done a reet grand job and we put Tommy in the stable, so Dad could see him when he got home from work. That done, Mam told me that I could go back to school.

"But, Mam", I started to say, but the look that she instantly put on her face reminded me that you didn't argue with Mam, so off I went. I was not in any hurry though and laiked around a bit, so, by the time I got back to school, we only had about ten minutes left of the lesson.

No sooner had I sat down than Clive leant over and whispered in my ear.

"We are going to get bashed after school, by the lads in the next class."

"Eh, what for?"

"Because all the lasses were hanging around us and Tommy," he told me.

"But we didn't ask the lasses to hang around us" I said.

"I know, that's what I told 'em, but they're still going to bash us." Clive said with a shrug.

The bell rang to say lessons had finished and, for the first time in our school days, Clive and me hung back. Unheard of as it was, we were the last out of the classroom.

"What are we going to do, Joe? I can see them waiting for us." Clive said, as we slowly headed for the door.

"I'm not going to let them bash me, I'm going to hit them first" I told him, sounding a lot more confident than I felt.

With that, we both ran out of the classroom, straight up to the lads who were gathered, waiting, and hit two of them in the face, bursting their noses. The other lads just stood and looked at us. Clive and me stood our ground, ready to react should any of them take a swing at us, but the stand-off was short lived, as the headmaster came striding out into the playground.

"Sawley and Paley, come here. I have just seen you attack those two lads for no reason at all!"

"But Sir, they were going to hit us" we both cried out.

"Come to my office, immediately!" With that, the headmaster turned and strode back into the school.

We knew it would be the cane and that no amount of trying to explain would help us. We walked back into the school and to his office even slower than we had walked out of the classroom.

We each got two whacks of the cane and that was our first experience of the dangers of getting involved with lasses!!

18
THE COWHEEL

Summer was a busy time on the farm and hay making was the most important job. We needed a good crop of hay so that we could feed the animals through the winter months. Our Tommy was having to work long hours, to make sure that everything that had to be done got done.

The farm's 28 acres comprised of a number of small, dry stone walled fields. The land though was poor, with thin, acid soil barely covering the underlying boulder clay and grit stone. If that wasn't enough, it was also hilly, which made working the land extremely hard for both Dad and Tommy.

Sometimes, when I was putting Tommy back in the stable after a day's work, he would be absolutely soaked in sweat, with his mouth dripping with lather. Dad was pleased with Tommy and quite often I heard him telling Mam what a good strong horse he was and how he was just what we needed on the farm. Even if Dad hadn't kept reminding us, we all knew how important Tommy was to the success of the farm, so I'd give him a good rub down and feed him his favourite food - oats. Comfortable again, Tommy would then settle for the night and, by morning, he would be fully rested and ready for another day's work.

We had no mower to cut the grass. That, Dad told us, was to be his big buy for next summer. This meant that Jonas Stephenson would oblige and cut the grass that year, as he had for the previous few years. Jonas was a farmer from further up Treacle Lane and he had a mower machine and tractor, which was a whole lot easier than cutting the grass with Tommy! I knew he liked coming to our farm, because of the good dinner that he always got. One day, I heard him tell our Mam,

"Missus, tha's best cook in Cowling. Eh by gum, that dinner was fair grand, it'll put me up for t'day, not like some of the farms I go to."

I watched him tapping his nose whilst he said that last part of his sentence, without having a clue at the time as to what he was doing it for.

Everyone had to help at hay making time, Denis, Ada and me. Denis would get a bit awkward if Dad wanted him to help on a Saturday night, as that was when he wanted to go courting. He was sweet on one of the lasses that lived on Treacle Lane, but he had a few to choose from, as a lot of the lasses in the village fancied him. I don't know if it was the fact that he had thick black hair and plastered it with Brylcream, or whether it was because he looked and dressed a bit flash, which was different to the other local farm lads, but, either way, it worked.

Anyway, whether Denis liked it or not, hay-making took priority over just about everything. I've got to admit, as tiring as the haymaking was, when it was finally finished, it was nice to see the barn full of sweet smelling hay. It also meant that I was once more able to go and laik with Clive. We'd meet down in the village and, with it being summer and light till late, we could stay out a bit later, before Clive would go home with his sister and I would go home with Madge.

Our favourite place was the fish shop, where just about all of the kids would hang out. Clive and I would often go in and get a pennies worth of chips, to share. One night, when we went into the shop, we saw that Henry was being served. Now, Henry was noted for liking the beer and, that night, he was lurching from side to side, as he purchased a cowheel.

For those of you who don't know, a cowheel is pretty much what the name suggests, a cow's foot, which was salted and boiled.

Clutching his cowheel, partially wrapped in newspaper, Henry staggered out of the shop. Me and Clive got our chips and, as we went back outside, we saw him walking not far in front of us.

Now, when I say walking, I'm being kind, because he was having great difficulty just standing up! On his feet was a pair of old cut-down wellingtons. He just looked so funny that, walking just a couple of yards behind him, Clive and me were laughing and giggling so much that we were nearly choking on our chips.

"Clear off, you young sods!" Henry shouted. "You're not having my cowheel!"

Suddenly, in the middle of his ranting, Henry dropped the greasy cowheel and we watched, as it slipped down into the inside of one of his wellingtons. We now couldn't have stopped laughing even if we'd wanted to.

Henry then became extremely abusive, swearing and cursing and threatening us with the police for stealing his cowheel. Through our laughing, we tried to tell him that it was in his wellington, but he just continued ranting and swearing. Henry's drunken behaviour continued as he lurched on, towards his house. If anything, as he approached his house, his cursing grew even louder.

Just then, out of a narrow ginnal, the local bobby appeared. Henry, swaying alarmingly in front of him, drunkenly told him that we'd stolen his cowheel. The bobby looked down at me and Clive, both of us still grinning like Cheshire cats.

"Stealing is no laughing matter boys!" He sternly advised us.

"We didn't steal it," we protested, "he dropped it and it fell into his wellie!"

Despite having the policeman glowering down at us, as we said this we couldn't help but start to laugh again. The bobby looked at Henry's boot, then back at us, then at Henry's boot again, as the start of a smile started to show on his face.

"Henry, your cowheel is in your Wellington," the bobby told him, struggling to get the words out without laughing.

Henry gave him a puzzled look, and then started to reach down. It was lucky for him that the bobby was holding him, or he would have fallen flat on his face, but, with a lot of effort, Henry finally got his hand inside his wellington and, when, several seconds later, he pulled it back out, he was holding the cowheel. The look of confusion on his face was soon replaced by a drunken grin, before he lifted the cowheel to his face and started to eat it.

"It's alright lads, I'll lead him home," the bobby told us. "Come on Henry, your wife's waiting for you!"

At the mention of his wife, Henry suddenly went very quiet, seemed to shiver, and even started to walk a little straighter.

Later, as I was going home, I was still laughing about Henry and couldn't wait to tell everyone the story. I went into the farmhouse all ready to launch into my story, but, even as I opened the door, I could hear Mam coughing repeatedly. She had been coughing like this for a week or two and, because Mam was never ill, we'd all noticed it.

As Mam's coughing fit continued, Dad said that maybe she should go and see the Doctor. The coughing fit easing, Mam cleared her throat before answering him.

"Don't be daft, it's nowt and anyway, it'll cost 8/6 to see him. I've plenty of stuff in t'cupboard to cure me cough."

It was certainly true that the cupboard was full of Mam's home-made remedies. It didn't matter what you had, constipation, sickness, diarrhoea, fever, coughs, whatever we had, out came one of Mam's remedies. None of them had the best taste in the world, but we were told 'get it down you, it will do you good!' To this day I remember 'Fenning's Fever Cure' it was horrible and, even now, whenever I think about it I can still taste it.

After Mam's latest coughing fit and the discussion that followed, I completely forgot to tell everyone about Henry's cowheel.

19
A New Class and Guests For Tea

When we returned to school after the summer holidays, Clive and I were in a new class, Standard 3, with a new teacher, Mrs Laycock, who happened to be the headmaster's wife. We were leaving Mrs Scott behind and neither of us were going to shed a tear about that.

Norman had already left the school and now attended the Grammar school in Keighley, whilst Madge had moved to a school in Crosshills. Not having Norman around meant that Clive, Maurice and me felt a bit lost back at school, after all, he was three years older than us and we sort of looked up to him. On top of that, we had been laiking with him through the summer holidays and had got used to all being together.

Overall though, as we arrived at school on that first day back, we were happy, because we wouldn't have Mrs Scott shouting at us. Our happiness was misplaced and short-lived. Going from having Mrs Scott to having Mrs Laycock as our teacher, was like jumping out of the frying pan into the fire. She had long pointed nails and, as we soon found out, when she got hold of you round the neck, to drag you out from your desk, her nails seemed to bite your neck.

Me and Clive came to the conclusion that all teachers were told to be horrible to kids at school. We still had our slop monitors job, though, so we did get out of the classroom during the afternoon. We always tried to make the job last about an hour and, when Mrs Laycock asked us one day why we took so long, we went to great lengths to explain to her that the galvanised iron pails were very heavy and full to the top with the smelly waste food and we had to go slowly, as we didn't want to spill any on the road.

"Do you think she believed us?" Clive whispered in my ear. I just nodded my head and hoped that she did.

Mrs Laycock wasn't my only problem at school. It was common knowledge amongst the kids at school that my parents weren't married. Regularly I would face taunts from some of the boys about Mam and Dad living o'er the brush. I didn't really understand what the fuss was about but, loving my Mam and Dad like I did, I would quickly get angry at anybody sniggering about them, or talking sneeringly about them and, as a result, I would regularly get involved in fights.

This fighting would see me being sent to see the headmaster, who would cane me and make me stay back after school. This was bad enough, but the fact is that being caned and given detention was only part of my punishment. You see, I didn't want to upset my Mam by telling her I'd been fighting and had been made to stay after school, because I'd have to tell her why I'd been fighting. So, when she asked why I was late home, I'd lie and tell her that I'd been laiking with the other boys after school. This in turn would see Mam shout at me about how many times she'd told me to come straight home after school. The harsh sound of her words would be joined by the sharp slap of her hand against my face. I couldn't win.

Life at Pondhill continued pretty much the same as always, with Mam looking after the farm and Dad going out to work. Sometimes I would hear Dad say to Mam that when he retired they could look after the farm together and it would be reet grand.

Aunts, uncles and cousins continued to regularly visit. They would sit around the pine table, in front of the blazing fire, their plates piled high with Mam's mouth-watering stews, or homemade pies, filling their bellies and washing all the food down with a pot of tea. When it came to the time for them to leave, Mam, as usual, would send them on their way weighed down with bags full of cheese, eggs, ham and potatoes. This still occasionally caused Dad to be grumpy and to grumble to Mam, telling her that it was food we could not afford to give away, but, as always, Mam would just say that we had to look after family.

Denis had got himself a girlfriend, but he never brought her to the farm. This upset Mam, who thought that it meant that Denis was a bit ashamed of the farmhouse and of her and Dad, and that they weren't good enough for him to bring his girlfriend to meet them.

Now Ada was different. She too was courting, a man called John and one Sunday he came for tea. What a to-do, Mam was scrubbing, cleaning and baking all week getting ready for him and then, as Sunday approached, the tab rug came out.

"Give over love, he's not royalty" Dad said exasperatedly.

"Well, we want to make a reet good impression on him" Mam informed Dad.

Sunday arrived and Mam was in a reet flummox, telling me and Madge, over and again, what to do and what not to do. I was beginning to wonder who this John was. Then, all of a sudden, he arrived with Ada, in a car! Not 'just' a car either, but a Ford 10. No wonder Mam was making a fuss, no-one had ever been to the farm in a car before.

They had hardly got out of the car before I asked if I could sit in it. Before either of them could reply, Mam told me that I couldn't.

Like everyone else, I was watching John closely. He was medium height, a bit thin and he had blond hair. When Ada introduced him to Mam and Dad he shook hands with them. I thought he must be posh and I thought Mam was going to curtsy to him. Anyway, Mam had made a reet spread, with ham salad, fruit cake, buns and apple pie and cream. John said that he had never seen such a table, and then he didn't half tuck in. When he'd finally eaten his fill, he said it was the best meal he had ever had. Mam went a bit pink, but I knew that she was happy that he had enjoyed his tea.

While we were all still sat around the table, John asked Dad how things were going on the farm. During this conversation, Dad mentioned that it was time he arranged for Mr Binns to bring his boar to visit again, to brim the sow.

The words were out of my mouth before I even realised that I was saying them.

"Our Denis is like a boar, he was brimming a lass in the hay shed."

Everyone's gaze was fixed on me as a stunned silence swept around the table. Finally, the sound of a loud, sharp slap filled the air and echoed off the walls. As I heard the noise of the slap reverberating, I realised that my head was stinging and saw Mam's hand retreating having fulfilled its mission.

"Joe Sawley, you get up to your room this minute!"

I didn't understand what I'd done wrong, but it was obvious that Mam was far from happy with me.

Later, when Ada and John had left to go to the pictures, I heard Mam and Dad talking.

"Eh, our Ada wants to stick hold a'that John, he's getten his own house and car and a job in t'mill" Mam told him.

"Now love, leave 'em to it", came Dad's reply, but Mam had to have the last word,

"Tha' haven't seen a lot a'fellas around here with a house and car. I'm telling you, our Ada wants to stick to him".

20
ADA GETS MARRIED

When you're young, you tend to accept things as they are and expect them to stay the same, so I didn't always notice straight away the changes that were taking place at the farm. I had always been used to Mam baking our bread, so it came as a surprise when Mam told me to go with her to the baker's van one day, as she had to buy some bread.

"But you always bake our bread Mam," I said "Why do we need a loaf from the baker?"

"What with all the other things that need doing on the farm, it's getting a bit much for me to make our own bread." Mam told me, as we set off to walk along Treacle Lane.

The baker, Matthew Lumb, from Colne, called at the top of Treacle Lane every Thursday in his bakery van. As well as bread, it was full of fancy cakes, suet cakes and flat cakes and before you even stepped into it, you were met by the most wonderful smell that made your mouth water. Once you stepped inside the van, the sight of all of the fantastic cakes made your eyes join forces with your nose, so that as well as your mouth watering, your stomach would cry out to be allowed to enjoy one of them.

Every Thursday, when he pulled up in his van, Mr Lumb would blow the van's horn. It was just like what happened in the pied piper – as soon as he blew that horn farmers wives and kids would come from everywhere, irresistibly drawn to the van. Some of them came just to look, others to buy bread, whilst, if it was a birthday, some would buy a cake.

That day, when Mam and me got to the van, she bought 10 loaves, but no cakes, because there was never enough money to afford fancy cakes. As we turned to leave the van, Mr Lumb called me back and gave me a jam tart. I think it was because Mam had bought so much bread, but, whatever the reason, I didn't care as I wolfed it down in case he changed his mind.

As we were walking back along Treacle Lane to the farm, loaded up with the 10 loaves, I asked Mam why, all of a sudden, we needed so much bread.

"You cloth head, I have to make bait every day for Father, Denis and Ada to take to work," Mam told me.

Until then, I hadn't realised just how much bread Mam used to have to bake every week, no wonder she didn't have the time to do it.

From then on, after school every Thursday, the bakery van would be parked on Treacle Lane and it was my job to help Mam to get the bread and carry it back to the farm. I looked forward to it, because every week Mr Lumb would give me a jam tart, but, being a kid, it wasn't long before I started to expect to be given a jam tart every week and to wish that he'd give me one of the mouth-watering fancy cakes instead.

As I said, youngsters don't tend to notice change, so you'll not be surprised that, in my mind, other than the introduction of the baker's van, life on the farm continued as per usual. That is, until one supper time when we were all, as usual, sat eating at the kitchen table and Ada said that she had something to tell us. With that, she announced that her and John were getting married and it was happening the following week.

There was a stunned silence for a few seconds, during which I saw that Mam and Dad were looking at each other.

"That's a bit sudden," Mam sounded shocked, but continued, "Art thou in pudding club?"

"No, I'm not!" Ada said sharply. "We've been courting a year."

The three of them, Mam, Dad and Ada were all looking at each

102

other, as an uncomfortable silence descended.

"What's pudding club?" I asked of no-one in particular.

"Wilt tha' shut up and eat tha' supper" Dad told me, glaring at me as he said it.

I knew better than to say anything else, so I shut up and ate my supper, but I told myself that I'd ask Norman about the pudding club, he'd be bound to know.

"Mam, you will come to the wedding won't you?" Ada asked, before confirming "it's at Keighley Registry Office."

"Ah love, it would make my day to see thee wed, but I don't have a decent dress or coat." Mam told her.

"We can manage a dress and coat if you want to go to wedding, love," Dad immediately told Mam. "You go and buy something, Ada will go with you" Dad continued, making it plain that if Mam wanted to go to the wedding she would be wearing a new outfit.

"No, I would never wear the dress again and the money could be better spent on something else," Mam insisted, in her 'I've made my mind up and don't bother arguing with me' voice.

"I know," she went on, "we will have a reet good slap up tea when tha' gets back from the Registry office. Does tha' think that's a better idea?"

Without thinking, I chipped in "Having summat to eat is best idea."

I just managed to move my head quick enough to avoid my earhole being met by Mam's hand, as she told me, in no uncertain terms, that she was talking to Ada, not me.

So it was agreed, on the Saturday of the wedding, we would have a slap up feed.

There was still time for some upset before the wedding, though. Our Ada came home from work one day in floods of tears. Mam calmed her down and asked her what was wrong.

"The girls at the mill say that they've heard that I'm in the pudding club. Someone's told them that that's why me and John are getting married so quickly. How can people be so cruel?" she sobbed.

"I wish I knew who'd started that rumour," said Mam, "I'd have something to say to them. Now don't you worry, our Ada, time will show that you're not in t'pudding club and will put paid to the rumour."

Now, in my defence, all that I had done was to ask Norman what being in the pudding club meant. He said that he didn't have a clue and asked me why I wanted to know, so I told him that our Ada had announced that she was getting married next Saturday.

"Heck, that's a bit quick," Norman said.

"That's what our Mam said," I told him. "And then she asked Ada if she was in the pudding club and, when I asked what it meant, they told me to shut up."

"I'll ask me Mam, she'll know" Norman reassured me.

So, he did and next thing you know, all the mill girls have heard about Ada being in the club.

Not only did I not even realise that I'd started the rumour, I still didn't know what being in the pudding club meant! I'm just glad that Mam and Ada never knew that it was me – I don't know what they'd have done, but I know it would have hurt!

Mam and Madge didn't stop all week. Baking, cleaning, more baking and cleaning again. By the Saturday morning of the wedding, the farmhouse was spotless and, as the final touch, Mam's tab rug was brought out and put in position.

The kitchen table was full of food and by gum it looked good. There was home-cured ham, rabbit pie, jacket potatoes, cabbage, carrots and Mam's homemade apple pie.

Dad did his bit, bringing out a bottle of Mam's homemade elderberry wine that was left over from Christmas. Mam looked over everything and gave a satisfied nod, which meant that we were ready.

Ada and John arrived back after the wedding with Madge, who had been a bridesmaid, Denis, Aunt Maggie, who had never been known to miss a good, free feed and Uncle Brian.

When they walked into the farmhouse and looked at the table, John turned to Mam and said

"I hope Ada feeds me as well as you feed your family, Mother-in-law, what a feast, it's fit for a king."

Everyone was talking and laughing, as, between us, we did our best to get rid of any evidence that Mam had been baking all week! When Dad put an arm around Mam and told her 'tha's done 'em proud, love', Mam beamed with pride.

All too soon it was time for Ada and John to leave. They were going to Blackpool, which to me, who'd hardly been anywhere and certainly nowhere as far away as Blackpool, sounded really exciting, like a foreign country.

We all went outside to say goodbye and wave them off, when, just as John and Ada were getting into John's car, Aunt Maggie called out to him.

"We can't walk down to the bus stop, it being such a long way. Can we get in with you two, after all, you have plenty of room in the back of the car."

Aunt Maggie was right, there was loads of room, so I didn't understand why John looked far from pleased as he told Maggie and Brian to get in the car.

When everyone had left, Madge and I noticed that Mam looked tired, so we told her to sit down and we would wash up.

So Mam and Dad both sat in front of the range, the fire blazing in the grate, as it was still early in the year and you needed a fire in the farm house.

Mam was smiling, as she kept saying to nobody in particular, "Who would have believed our Ada would marry a fellow who had his own house and a car!"

"You gave them a good send off, but I don't know if our Ada will feed John like you feed us!" Dad said and we all burst out laughing.

It was nice to see Mam and Dad sat together, happy in each other's company. It would be something that I would often remember in the years to come.

21
MAM BECOMES ILL

For two years Mam had not been very well, but she wouldn't go to the doctor because, she said it cost too much money. Even when Dad pointed out that doctors' treatment was now free, she was still adamant that she wasn't going to the doctors.

"I can cure myself" I often heard her say and, as I've said before, it was no good arguing with Mam. Mam didn't wear stockings and one day I noticed that her legs were bleeding. I told her, but she just said that it was nothing. Over the next few weeks I noticed it happening more and more, but still Mam insisted that it was nothing and that she could cure herself. After a few weeks of listening to Mam denying that the bleeding meant there was anything really wrong with her and with her having taken to her bed, Dad, more aware than the rest of us that Mam was not at all well, called the doctor.

The news was not good. The doctor told Dad that he should have called him weeks ago and that Mam would have to go to hospital. The doctor told Dad that an ambulance would be there within an hour, and then he left. We were all really upset but, as much as I wanted to cry, I didn't want Mam to see how upset I was.

Dad tried to get Mam downstairs, ready for when the ambulance arrived, but she was a big woman and he had to go and ask for help from the farmer next door. Ken Wilcox and his wife Edna had only moved into the farm next to ours a few weeks before. Ken was a big chap and very strong, whilst Edna was similar to Mam, home loving and kind. I didn't know it then, but they would become like family to Madge and me.

Ken came back with Dad and, between them, they managed to get Mam downstairs. When the ambulance arrived, it couldn't get down to the farm from the lane, so Dad had to put Mam in a chair and wrap her in a blanket, before he and Ken could carry her up to the waiting ambulance. I watched as the ambulance drove off, tears rolling freely down my cheeks. Dad put his arms around Madge and me and, having thanked Ken for his help, walked us back to the farm.

When we walked back inside, I swear that the house was colder without Mam in it, but Dad said that we shouldn't worry, as Mam would get better now that she was in hospital and would soon be fine. I know he was trying to cheer us up, but I could see how worried Dad was.

With Mam away, there was a lot of work that had to be covered by the rest of us. Dad said that Madge and me would have to feed the hens, of which we now had about 200 and the pig, while he would milk the 3 cows before he went to work and then again when he got home from work. The problem was that milking the cows was time consuming and Dad wanted to go and visit Mam in hospital, so, it was decided that I had to learn how to milk cows.

Madge was doing the washing and cooking while Mam was in hospital, but, despite her efforts, by the time the following Monday came round, I had no clean trousers.

"What am I going to wear to school?" I asked Madge, who came up with the idea of cutting down one of Dad's old boiler suits. She cut down the legs and arms and I put a belt round my waist and pulled it tight, to stop the suit from being too baggy. With that done, I set off for school, feeling quite grown up, as after all, lots of folk wore boiler suits.

As I arrived at school Clive didn't say a word, just looked at me. We went into the classroom and sat down. Straight away I started to tell Clive about Mam going into hospital, but, before I'd said more than a few words, Mrs Laycock, our teacher, came in and we all stood up and said good morning. Even as she was saying good morning to everyone she looked at me and her face darkened.

"What are you wearing, Joe Sawley?" she shouted.

Every pair of eyes in the class room turned to look at me, there was total silence for a couple of seconds, which was broken when one of the kids laughed. This acted like a trigger, as it seemed to me that everyone else then started to laugh and point at me. Only Clive was quiet.

"Be quiet!" Mrs Laycock bellowed and the laughter stopped as suddenly as it had begun.

"You do not come into my classroom in a boiler suit. You look like a clown. Take it off now!" Mrs Laycock had a face like thunder as she spat her orders at me with venom.

There was no way I could take off the boiler suit. All I had on underneath it were vest and underpants, so I just sat there.

"Do you hear me?" she roared.

I knew that just sitting still and saying nothing wasn't an option, so I looked at her and took a deep breath.

"I'm not taking it off" I heard the words spoken in my voice, but my face looked as stunned as those of all the other kids, because we all knew that no-one ever answered a teacher back.

The disbelief that a pupil had answered back to her hardly had time to settle on her face before it was replaced by pure fury.

"How dare you answer me back!" she screamed, as her face continued to twist and snarl in anger.

"You, a …a… farm boy dare to answer me, the headmaster's wife and class teacher, back! Stay where you are Sawley, I'm going for the headmaster!" Her eyes were bulging and her face went through a range of colours, settling on purple, as she screeched at me, turned on her heel and stomped out of the door.

An eerie silence filled the classroom, as though everyone was holding their breath, afraid to be the first to make a sound.

Finally, Clive said in a low voice "What are you going to do, Joe?"

"I'm going home" I said, as I ran out of the classroom and headed for the school gate.

This was my last year at this school and I was glad, I hated it. I ran all the way home and burst through the door into the kitchen, where I stopped in my tracks. The fire was out in the grate and the kitchen was cold and quiet. This was the first time I had come home from school and Mam was not there working in the kitchen. I sank down onto the old horsehair sofa and cried, I had never felt so lonely in my life.

I don't know how long I'd been sat on the sofa crying, but I suddenly felt cold and, as I shivered, I thought of Mam. I knew what she would say, I could hear it in my head, "Get up off your backside young Joe, light the fire and stop blubbering". The thought of what Mam would say made me smile and, as I got up to see to the fire, I felt better and smiled as I started to think about how Mam would soon be coming home.

By the time Denis, Madge and Dad arrived home, I had fed the hens and the pig and managed to milk the cows. Tommy was out in the fields now that the weather was getting warmer, so he was fine and the fire in the grate was glowing, making the kitchen feel a little warmer. Dad was pleased, because it meant that he had time to go and see Mam, but he was puzzled as to how I had done all the farm work after school and asked me how I'd managed it. I didn't answer straight away and then, as he was looking at me, he suddenly noticed what I was wearing.

"Don't tell me you went to school like that! What happened?" he wanted to know, so I had to tell him.

"Madge, how could you send lad to school like that?" he said, after I'd told him what had happened that morning. "You've made us a laughing stock."

All Madge could do was to say was how sorry she was. Dad told

Madge not to worry, but to go into town on Saturday to get some decent clothes for me. Then he said that he would write a note to the teacher, explaining that Mam was in hospital and young Joe needed to be at home for the next few days. I said that I would feed the hens and the pig and milk the cows in the evening, so that Dad could go and see Mam and Dad smiled and said that Madge and I could go with him to the hospital one night later in the week, when Mam felt a bit better.

I was glad not to be going back to school for the next few days, but it made me realise how hard Mam worked on the farm. She looked after the animals, the farmhouse, the cooking, the washing and the cleaning, and all of that with none of the modern appliances that people have got these days. For washing the clothes she had two large galvanised tubs, a brass poser on a long wooden handle and a big heavy mangle with large wooden rollers. To clean the stone flags on the kitchen floor, which she did every day, she would get down on her knees and scrub until every bit of dirt had disappeared.

At last Saturday arrived, which meant Dad and Denis would do most of the farm work. I was tired and glad Madge was taking me into town for some new clothes. I think we went into every shop in town looking for a pair of pants and a jacket for me. I did think Madge was trying to save some of the money, so she could buy something for herself, but she said she was just looking for a bargain. After several hours we were finally done and headed home. I had two pairs of pants, a jacket, two shirts and a tie. They were all too big for me, but Madge informed me that I would grow into them.

When we arrived home, Dad was pleased with what we had bought and said that we could go and see Mam the next day, Sunday. I was excited, not only because we were going to see Mam, but also because she must have been getting better, as we were being allowed to go and see her.

On Sunday afternoon we all set off to go and see Mam, me feeling all proud and smart in my new clothes. I'd never had new clothes before and I wondered what Mam would think about Dad spending all that money on me. At last the bus arrived at the hospital. I'd never been to the hospital before and when I saw it I felt a bit scared, but Dad told me not to worry. He said he would go in first to see Mam and then take in Madge and me. After he'd been in to see Mam for about ten minutes, Dad came and got us and took us onto the ward.

I looked around in amazement, there were beds all the way along both sides of the ward and all of them full. There were people coughing, people sleeping and others shouting for the nurse. I was still taking all of this in, when we got to Mam's bed. I saw Mam and threw myself into her arms and burst into tears. I was so happy to see her, but she looked so ill and thin.

"Now young Joe, let me have a look at you all dressed up in your new clothes. My, you are looking smart" Mam beamed at me.

"When are you coming home, Mam? The house is not the same when you are not there." I sobbed. "When the doctor lets me out" Mam told me, hugging me again.

Mam told me that I had to go to school and she told Madge to keep an eye on me. Just talking to us was too much for her and soon a nurse came over and told us that Mam needed to rest and we had to leave. I didn't want to leave, but Madge and me hugged and kissed Mam goodbye and, waving as we went, left the ward. Dad followed a few minutes later.

For all that I was upset that we weren't able to take Mam home with us that day, I was happy that Dad had taken us to the hospital to see her. I knew that I'd missed Mam terribly, but hadn't realised just how much until I'd seen her, hugged her and talked with her.

Little did I realise as we waved our goodbyes that that would be the last time I would ever see my Mam.

22
WE SAY GOODBYE TO MAM

The morning after we'd visited Mam, I woke up far from happy. Not only was I really worried about Mam and how ill she had looked, but it was Monday morning and that meant I had to go back to school and face Mrs Laycock.

As usual, I met Clive at the school gate and he wanted to know how Mam was. I told him about the hospital visit and how worried I was about Mam, and then he told me that Mrs Laycock had gone crackers when she arrived back in the classroom with the headmaster to find me no longer there. That did nothing to improve how I was feeling.

So I went into the classroom fully expecting to be sent straight to the headmaster for the cane, but when the teacher came in she didn't say a word to me and the morning passed off quietly. At play time, even though it was only the 30th April, Clive, Maurice and me were talking about the new schools that we would go to after the summer holidays. Maurice would be going to the grammar school in Keighley, whilst Clive and I would go to Cross Hills secondary school. We were all excited about our new schools, but I knew that I still had a few months of Mrs Laycock to get through before then, so I didn't let myself get too excited. Despite my fears, the next few days passed off quietly at school, with Mrs Laycock ignoring me, which suited me just fine. I just kept my head down and got on with my work as best as I could, given that I couldn't stop thinking about Mam and how I couldn't wait for her to be better and back at Pondhill.

Just over a week later my life changed forever. It was on Wednesday

9th May 1951 that I arrived home from school to find Ada and John waiting for me. I looked round and saw that Madge was sat on the sofa crying and, before anyone said anything, I knew.

"Oh no, it's not Mam" I cried.

Ada came over, put her arms around me and told me that our beloved Mam had gone. After suffering lengthy bouts of bronchitis and pneumonia, Mam had sadly passed away in the hospital that morning. She was only 59. Dad had been with Mam at the hospital at the end and had returned home with the news that none of us wanted to hear.

My world suddenly fell apart. My life, our lives and life at Pondhill would never be the same again. I felt like my heart was going to burst as, grief stricken, I raced out of the farmhouse and into the mistel, crying uncontrollably. I could hear the muffled sound of sobbing coming from one of the stalls and found Dad there, hunched over one of the timber stalls, in floods of tears.

My Dad, who had always been this tall, well-built man. A hard, muscular Yorkshire man, a tough engineer and hill farmer. This man who I had never ever seen shed even the slightest tear, was now slumped in front of me, barely recognisable as the man I knew, totally distraught. Going over to him, I wrapped my arms around his waist, hugging him as tight as my little arms could, both of us sobbing uncontrollably. Dad had not only lost his dearly beloved wife, but his best friend, and Madge and I had lost our wonderful, loving Mam.

For the next few days, people called at the farm, expressing their condolences. Aunts, uncles, farmers and people from the village all came and went, then, suddenly, it was the day of Mam's funeral. I got up early, feeling heartbroken and totally forlorn, but determined to help Dad feed our flock of over 200 hens.

Mary, our cow, had produced a number of calves, who were out grazing the spring grass in the meadows. Tears slipped down my cheeks as I could hear Mam's voice telling me that May was the time of year to turn the stock out into the fields. "It's far more profitable that the cows and pigs eat grass rather than us having to buy costly proven" she would tell me.

After feeding the hens, I carried several buckets of water from the well into the kitchen, filling up the set-pot attached to the range. The fire in the range would heat the water in the set-pot, giving us hot water for washing, etc. Madge had also risen early and was making breakfast, ready for when Dad had finished the milking. However, when Dad came into the kitchen he looked ghastly, his face completely drained of colour. He said he didn't fancy having breakfast and would just have a pint pot of tea. I realised that I couldn't face the thought of eating either, so just had a glass of milk.

Dad had hardly said anything since our Mam's death. Madge and I could hear him sobbing every night when he was in bed and, hearing him grieving made Madge and me cry even more.

After he had drunk his tea, Dad and Madge were getting washed and dressed ready for Mam's funeral. I told Dad that I would wear my new pants and jacket, as I wanted to look smart for Mam. Dad and Madge looked at each other, and then back at me.

"What's up" I said.

"Sorry young Joe lad, but you can't go to the funeral, it will be far too upsetting for you."

Dad quietly told me this and then explained that some of our relatives had said that I was too young and shouldn't be allowed to attend. Who were they to interfere? I was so hurt and felt totally dejected and utterly miserable. How could they not let me go to Mam's funeral?

Looking back, I'm sure that the family acted with the best intentions, as they could see how our Mam's death had affected me.

"But Dad, I have to go, I want to go, I loved my Mam!" My eyes were full of tears as I pleaded.

Dad, placed an arm around my shoulders and gave me a tender hug, but still said no. Pulling away from Dad I ran, sobbing, out of the kitchen into the yard, where I bumped straight into Maurice, who was walking across the yard. He said that his Mam had sent him over to keep me company until after the funeral.

"So your Mam knew before me that I wouldn't be allowed to attend my Mam's funeral" I said, tears cascading down my face.

Sitting with Maurice on the roof of the pigeon hut at Court House Farm, I looked on tearfully as the gleaming black hearse carrying Mam's coffin quietly drove by on its way down from Pondhill into Cowling. From there, the cortege drove up to Cock Hill graveyard, situated high on the windswept moors above Keighley.

I knew that after the funeral all the family, friends and neighbours would come back to the farm for tea and sandwiches, so, after leaving Maurice, I decided not to return home. Instead, feeling terribly sad and lonely, and missing Mam so desperately that it physically hurt, I walked over the moor to Cuckoo Rock.

Clambering up onto the top of this massive stone boulder, I sat down on its rough, hard surface and looked down from my elevated position to Pondhill. I think I must have cried myself to sleep, because I was awakened some time later by the cry of skylarks flying high above. I watched the acrobatic antics of the birds in flight until they disappeared, and then remained sitting on the rock, until it became quite dark.

When I finally got back to the farm, everyone had gone home. Madge placed her arms around me and asked me where I had been, as everyone had been worried.

"I just went up and sat on the Cuckoo Rock" was my reply.

Following Mam's funeral, me and Madge didn't go back to school for a week. On the Sunday morning, Madge and I told Dad we would carry out the washing of all the dirty clothes. Madge boiled kettles of water on the range and I dragged two galvanised dolly tubs into the kitchen. Madge filled one up with the hot water from the kettle, to wash the clothes in and filled the second one with cold water, to rinse the clothes.

We took it in turns stirring the clothes in the tub with the copper-headed posser. It was hard work, we would let the clothes soak in the soapy water for a few minutes, and then we would start possing again. Next, we would pass each item of clothing through the huge wood rollers of the mangle, winding the great big iron handle to make the rollers revolve and squeeze the water out of the clothing. Each piece of clothing was then rinsed in the cold water tub, which again involved us stirring the clothes with the posser, before each item was again put through the mangle. Operation completed, Madge carried the damp washing out to the yard to hang onto the washing line to dry.

Dad, came into the kitchen and, noticing the washing on the line, told us both that it was bad luck to hang washing out on a Sunday, saying that Mam always hung washing out on Mondays. Madge said that she would remember and, in future, would hang out the washing on Monday.

Madge asked Dad if she should remove Mam's tab rug, which was still in front of the range, having been put down for her funeral. Looking down at the rug, Dad said that he would prefer it to stay down. We noticed that from then on Dad would sit in front of the fire with his feet resting on the rug, I think the rug made him feel close to Mam.

The death of Mam was hard for all of us to come to terms with, but Dad was a broken man. Hardly eating, he was noticeably losing weight. True, Madge's cooking was not like Mam's, but she was trying and it wasn't bad. It wasn't just that though, he was so consumed in his grief that he rarely talked to us.

It was almost as though, as well as losing my Mam, I'd lost part of my Dad too. With Madge still herself only being a young girl and Ada being married and busy in her own life, there wasn't any adult to whom I could talk through my own grief and who could help me to face the huge hole in my life that losing Mam had caused.

Thank God for Clive, Norman and Maurice. Without any of us necessarily realising it at the time, their friendship was just about the only constant in my life in the months following Mam's death and, looking back, I don't know how I would have coped without it.

Denis had left the farm after Mam died, we didn't know why, but

I think he had a falling out with Dad. Things were really difficult and both Madge and I had to help on the farm before we went to school and when we got home after school every day. Then, a few months following Mam's passing, Dad told us that, as he was 65, he was going to retire from operating lathes at John Lund's. Madge and me were very pleased, as this would mean our workload would be reduced.

Dad appeared to settle down in his retirement. He still missed Mam, as we all did, and was still quite withdrawn, but he had a daily routine of milking the cows early in the morning, then feeding the hens and collecting the eggs. Mid-morning, he would attend to the important work of boiling pig-swill and, after mucking out the pigs, he would feed the freshly boiled swill to the ever-hungry porkers. In the afternoons he would see that we had plenty of firewood for the kitchen range, before milking the cows again after tea. I think he was beginning to settle in to full time farming and he didn't miss the long early morning walk to Cross Hills to work.

23
DAD FALLS ILL

After what seemed like a lifetime of waiting, the school bell finally rang on the last day that Clive and I had to go to Cowling School. We were eleven years old and six long weeks of summer lay ahead of us before we would start at our new school. As most of you will remember, when you're eleven years old, six weeks seems like forever, so, as we ran through the school gate that afternoon, as far as we were concerned we'd finished school.

I still desperately missed Mam, with little things every day reminding me just how much. When I arrived home from school every day, I missed the hug that used to greet me. Every time I walked through the kitchen, I missed the smell of the baking that she always seemed to be in the middle of. I also missed her cooking at meal times, when I would remember how much I loved the buns, pies and dinners that Mam made for us. Madge was really trying hard at cooking and baking, but it wasn't the same as Mam's.

As the weeks since we'd lost Mam passed, the three of us got into a routine for covering all of the work and jobs that had to be done around the house and farm. We all knew that the jobs on the farm had to be done every day and couldn't be left despite the fact that we were grieving. Besides, being kept busy all the time helped us to get back to some form of normality. As the summer progressed, Dad started to look and act more like his old self, which was a great relief to Madge and me.

As I stated before, Clive, Norman and Maurice helped me a lot coping with losing Mam and they spent even more time than usual with me throughout that summer. The three of them were regular, almost daily, visitors to Pondhill, which is more than could be said for others. The aunts, uncles and cousins who had been such regular visitors when Mam was there to ensure that they went home laden with food, were conspicuous by their absence. Not one of them paid even one visit - maybe it was Madge's cooking that put them off!

All too soon, the school holidays were over and it was time for Clive and I to start at our new school. Madge too was returning to school, but only until Christmas, when she was due to leave school and would be going out to work. She already had a job lined up at the mill and kept trying to tell me that she was looking forward to it, as she'd be earning money.

I was genuinely excited as I stood ready to go to school on that first morning. I was wearing a nice new shirt and tie, my new pants and my new jacket and I knew Mam would have been really proud to see me looking so smart. Not wanting to spoil my new look, I'd polished my clogs until they were as shiny as they'd ever been, they were that shiny that I could see my face in them – well, nearly.

Clive and I could not believe how nice all the teachers were at our new school. There was no being hit with a child's chair leg, no being pulled out to the front of the classroom by your hair, and the teaches didn't even look down on you just because you were poor. It was a different world to what we'd known before and we soon settled in and made some new friends, including Andrew and Peter.

Andrew Squires was a tall, lanky lad and was a bit posh. He lived in a big house and, not long after we got to know him, we discovered that his Mam & Dad had a greenhouse with a grape vine growing in it. Even now, thinking about those grapes makes my mouth water, by 'eck they were tasty. Several years later, Andrew went to work in Australia.

Peter Armitage was a fair haired, fairly short lad, who was always acting the fool. It was no surprise when, again years later, he became an actor in TV and films. Those amongst you who watch Coronation

Street will know him as Kevin Webster's father. Like so many of my friends from those days, our friendship has lasted the course of time and continues to this day.

Clive and I decided that, all things considered, we liked both the school and the teachers and the first term flew by without any incident of note. For a while, it looked like life, whilst busy, was going to enter a settled period for a change. I had no idea that tragedy hadn't finished with Pondhill and was about to visit us again.

My twelfth birthday and Christmas soon passed and 1952 began with me starting my second term and Madge starting work at the Mill. One day, as I got home from school, I opened the farm gate and could hear a loud bellowing coming from the mistel. I knew that it was Mary our cow, but I sensed that something was wrong, as she rarely made any noise, being a quiet and contented animal. I raced down the track and, as I approached the farmhouse, I could see that the kitchen door was open. I started shouting for Dad as I was running, but there was no answer and, I was starting to panic as I reached the door and ran straight in.

As I looked around the kitchen I was terrified to see that my Dad was slumped in the fireside armchair, still wearing his patched tweed jacket, with his cap askew on his head. My mind was racing, it looked like he was fast asleep, but the fire in the grate was out and Mam & Dad always kept the fire lit. As I took all this in I started shivering, and not just because the house was cold.

Feeling really frightened, I went up to the chair, telling myself over and over that Dad was just asleep.

"Dad, Dad wake up", I gently shook his shoulder.

He didn't wake, so with my fear growing, and with tears welling in my eyes, I grabbed his shoulder again and shook him harder.

"Wake up Dad, there's something wrong with Mary!"

Dad didn't stir, he just stayed slumped in his chair, looking like he was in a deep sleep.

I was so scared then, that I started shouting for Madge, running into the parlour to get her, before realising that she would be still at work. I was panicking now, but suddenly thought of Ken Wilcock next door, telling myself that he would know what to do. I ran out of the house and raced down the field to Ken's farm, Dean Laithe. Ken was working outside and heard me shouting before he could even see me running towards him.

"What's up, Joe?" he said.

"It's Dad", I gasped, "He's lying in a chair and I can't get him to wake up," my lungs were burning as I managed to splutter what had happened.

Ken shouted to his wife to look after me, and then set off running to Pondhill.

Mrs Wilcock took me into the farm house and told me to sit by the fire and she would make me a pot of tea. I was shaking like a leaf and still breathing hard, partly through running, but partly through fear and upset.

It seemed like hours before Ken came back. When he'd seen my Dad's obviously very poorly condition, he'd draped him in a blanket to keep him warm, then he'd ran to Mr Pollhard's farm, the only farm which had a telephone. After phoning for an ambulance, he'd ran back to Pondhill, getting there just as Madge was arriving home from work.

Ken told Madge what had happened and they both ran down the track and into the house. Madge was shocked to see Dad, slumped unconscious in the chair and, knowing that it was me who had found him, was worried about how I was. Ken said that he would go and fetch me, if Madge was okay staying with Dad.

When Ken arrived back at Dean Laithe, very much out of breath, I heard him tell his wife that he thought Dad had suffered a massive stroke. I didn't have a clue what that meant, but Ken then came over to me and, placing both hands on my shoulders, gently told me that my Dad was very ill.

"He's not going to die" I cried out, part as a question, part as a statement of defiance. All I wanted was my Dad to wake up.

"No lad, he's not, but an ambulance is on its way, as he needs to go to hospital" Mr Wilcock said reassuringly, but, as we ran back over to Pondhill, all I could think was that Mam went in an ambulance and never came home.

When I ran through the door into the farmhouse, Madge hurried over to me and we clung to each other, neither willing to let go of the other. After what seemed like forever, the ambulance arrived and Dad was lifted onto a stretcher before being carried up to the gate, where the ambulance waited. Ken told us that it would be better if he went with Dad in the ambulance, while Madge and me saw to the animals. We were too much in shock to raise any argument, so, once again, we stood and watched as a second member of our family left in an ambulance.

Having watched the ambulance until it disappeared, hand in hand we walked back down the lane back to the farm. Our minds were in turmoil, wondering about Dad and, despite everyone having told us that everything would be alright, we were both also wondering about what fate awaited us.

"What are we going to do, Madge?" I quietly asked, even though I dreaded the answer that I might get.

"We're going to feed the stock for Dad." Madge bravely replied, even as she was wiping the tears that were falling from her eyes.

I said that I would light the fire in the kitchen, milk Mary, and then feed the pigs, if Madge would feed the hens. Madge quickly agreed, especially to me feeding the pigs, which was a really smelly job which Madge hated. With the job split agreed, I ran upstairs and changed out of my school clothes, before setting the fire in the kitchen. With the fire lit, I headed straight to the mistel, where poor Mary was still making a racket, so desperate was she to be milked.

When we had finished all of our tasks, we sat having a cup of tea in front of the fire. The fire may have been blazing, but nothing could warm us, as we were engulfed by grief, fear and loneliness. As we sat there sobbing and holding each other, the door opened and John and Ada walked in. It turned out that, after Ken had used his phone to ring for an ambulance, Mr Pollhard had phoned the mill where John worked and had told him what had happened.

"We came as fast as we could," Ada said, bringing out a basket of meat pies, biscuits and bread. Although alerted by Mr Pollhard, they had not been given any detailed information. As Madge told them that we feared that Dad had suffered a stroke, John and Ada looked at each other, but didn't say anything. They joined Madge and myself, waiting for Ken to return from the hospital with an update on Dad's condition.

*

Dad never properly recovered from his stroke and remained at Burnley hospital for two long years.

In the days that followed, it became clear that, without Dad there, the stock would have to be sold. Whilst finally, and very reluctantly, accepting this, Madge and me were determined to stay at Pondhill. It was discussed by some of the relatives and, following this, one of the relatives said that Madge could live with them, but that they couldn't take me and I would be better off in a council run Boys Home. What they meant was, as Madge was working, they were willing to let her stay, no doubt in return for her handing over a sizeable proportion of her wages, whereas there was nothing in it for them where I was concerned, so they weren't interested.

I was horrified at the thought of being forced to leave Pondhill and even more horrified by the idea of being put into a Boys Home. I told Madge and Ada and was relieved to hear Madge telling everyone that we were both staying at Pondhill and that was final. Ada and John said that they would help as much as possible if we stayed and, with that, it was settled.

Whether or not anyone of us, at that time, realised that Dad would never return to Pondhill, I don't know. Certainly, when Madge and I were saying that we wanted to stay at Pondhill, I don't believe that either us, Ada, or anyone considered for a moment how long the current situation might continue.

Anyway, settled it was and, as two kids of 15 and 12, Madge and me were now living on our own at Pondhill.

As for the rest of the relatives? – realising that there was nothing in it for them, they left.

We never saw any of them visit Pondhill again.

24
Two New Best Friends – Meg and a Gun

Madge and I didn't realise how hard it would be staying at Pondhill. We had very quickly realised that the stock would have to be sold, but seeing Mary the cow, Tommy the horse, the pigs and the hens all leaving the farm gave me an emptiness in my stomach. I couldn't stop myself thinking about how hard Mam & Dad had worked, to make the farm habitable and then to stock it. They had sacrificed so much and gone without so much to make Pondhill work, and now all the stock had gone. I felt that the farm had died.

I went back to school, but loneliness consumed me when I came home each day and no-one was there, no fire was burning in the range and there was no smell of cooking. Even the fields were silent now that there were no animals in them. The sense of loss and of being lonely was so strong that I wondered if the feeling would ever leave me.

Hearing of Dad's illness, some of the villagers were really supportive. The local plumber's son rode up to Pondhill on a tandem and said that if I wanted it I could have it. I could not believe he was giving me the tandem and gratefully accepted. I was over the moon with my present. It was, in truth, far too big for me, but, after riding it around the yard a few times, I just about got the hang of being able to stay on it and make it go in the general direction that I wanted it to!

I was really excited and couldn't wait to show off the tandem to Clive and for us to plan all the things that it would allow us to do – the world would be our oyster now we had wheels!

What excited me most though was the fact that I'd be able to ride the tandem the thirteen miles over Cowling Moss, to visit Dad in hospital, meaning that I could go and see him more often. Until I had my wheels, if I wanted to visit Dad I had to go on the bus, which, at tuppence each way, was expensive. We only had Madge's wage coming in and, with money in short supply, tuppence each way for bus fares was an extravagance that we couldn't afford.

Occasionally, Clive would accompany me visiting Dad, riding on the back of the tandem, which made the twenty six mile round trip slightly easier. Riding up front, sometimes the trip seemed a lot harder than other times and, to this day, I still think there were times when he didn't pedal, although he always insisted that he had.

Madge was working long shifts at the mill, weaving cloth. For the first time in her life she was receiving a wage, but, instead of spending some of the money on food, she was spending it on dresses, skirts and jumpers. Madge had grown to be a tall, buxom, good looking blond lass and she'd soon made a good number of friends at the mill. She started to go out after work to the pictures and the like, not returning home until late and, within just a short period of time, it seemed to me as though she was out just about every night. I loved my sister and was glad that she was happy, but wished that she'd spent more of her wages on food for us and came home straight after work a lot more often than she did.

When Mam and Dad had been there, I used to like sitting in the evenings watching the shadows, formed by the fire and the candles, flicker and dance across the walls. Now, with neither Mam nor Dad there at the farm, the same shadows were scary and only served to remind me that I was all alone. I couldn't win, without the fire and candles burning, Pondhill was dark, bleak and really cold, but the more I built up the fire and lit candles, to try to make it look cosy, the more things creaked, the higher the shadows flickered and the more scared I became.

There were many nights when I was too frightened to stay in the farm house while I waited for Madge to come home, preferring to put on my hat and coat, stuff my feet into my wellies and go outside.

127

I'd hang about for hours in the pitch black at the farm gate, waiting for her. Often the weather would be freezing, but I preferred to stand there for two or more hours, waiting for Madge, rather than be alone in the farmhouse. It's strange, I wasn't at all afraid about being outside in the dark, but I couldn't stand being inside the farmhouse, alone, in the dark.

Despite my feeling so strongly about it, I didn't want Madge to know how afraid of being in the house I was. So, when I was waiting outside, as soon as I heard Madge walking up Treacle Lane, I would run back to the farmhouse and, still fully clothed, would jump into bed, pull the blankets over my head and pretend to be asleep.

I could never understand the reason Madge never spent much money on groceries for Pondhill. I suppose she ate her meals in the canteen at work and thought that, because I had school dinners, I was fine. Now I always ate my school dinner, but one meal a day just wasn't enough for me. I was hungry by the time that I arrived home from school, but the kitchen cupboards at Pondhill were nearly always bare.

To fend off my hunger pains, I would go round all the local farmers, seeing if anyone needed any odd jobs done. Usually, these jobs would earn me a few coppers, which would accompany me straight to the local chip shop. Mick and Muriel, like most of the other locals, were aware of our situation. They owned the chip shop and were extremely good to me, even though I didn't realise it at the time. It never struck me as strange that, just about every time I went in and asked for a penny's worth of chips, they always had either a fish, or a fishcake left over, which was going to go to waste, so would I like it. It wasn't until several years later that I realised that none of that food had been leftovers that were going to go to waste. Those wonderful people wanted to help me, but didn't want to embarrass me by asking if I wanted a hand-out.

One day when I went into the chip shop, Mick asked me if I would like a puppy. He told me that it was gun shy and, as he was a shooting man, it was no use to him and would be disposed of if I didn't want it.

Without waiting to hear my response, Mick disappeared into the back of the chip shop and, within seconds, returned holding a little puppy. I had instantly fallen in love with the little black cross Labrador puppy in his arms and barely heard Mick saying that he thought it could keep me company up there at Pondhill.

Again, at my young age, I didn't realise that Mick was lying to protect me from embarrassment and to disguise his and Muriel's incredible generosity. As such, I couldn't believe how lucky I was that one of the litter that Mick's bitch had delivered was gun shy and that he had to give it away. I kept thanking him and repeating how lovely she was, as Mick tied some string around it to act as a lead and then handed it to me. I was that excited that I could hardly eat my chips. I talked to her all the way back to Pondhill and told her that I was going to call her Meg.

Meg had a massive impact on my life, which started immediately. With my new best friend with me, I was no longer afraid about staying in the house by myself any more. Meg and me quickly became inseparable and, at night, we would cuddle up under the army blankets and keep each other warm.

One day soon after, after helping a local farmer to bring down his sheep off the moor, he asked if I wanted a single barrelled shot gun. He showed me the fifty year old gun and explained that it was no good to him, as the firing pin was missing, so it couldn't be fired. He told me that, whilst no longer any use as a real gun, it would be ideal for me to play cowboys and indians with it.

Arriving home, I was greeted by Meg and, as soon as she started sniffing at the gun, her tail started wagging so fast that I thought it was going to fall off. I was amazed - Meg was no longer gun shy!

"Come on Meg," I said, jumping up, "let's see if we can make a firing pin for the gun."

Rooting about in a box of nails and screws, I found a nail that looked to be about the size of the firing pin. I filed off the nail head and, picking up the gun and pushing the nail into place, I was thrilled to find that it fitted. Job done.

I was itching to fire the shot gun, so I went looking for Maurice and asked him if he could get me two cartridges from his Dad, who I knew had a gun. An hour later Maurice came across to Pondhill, bringing six cartridges with him.

"Six!" I said, "How did you get your Dad to give you six?"

"I didn't tell him," Maurice replied.

Both Meg and me looked worriedly at Maurice.

"Don't worry," he said, "Dad won't miss them, he's got hundreds of them."

That was good enough for me and, without wasting any more time, I took the shot gun up onto the moor. Seeing an empty pop bottle, I picked it up and placed it on top of a big, flat stone.

Meg stood nearby, watching intently as I loaded the gun and took aim.

I pulled the trigger and the pop bottle exploded with an enormous bang. I jumped up, cheering and shouting and Meg jumped around barking, both of us so excited that the home made firing pin had worked.

It didn't cross my mind until years later that, not only was using an improvised firing pin, made by a lad who had never even handled a gun before, extremely dangerous, but also the fact that the gun hadn't been fired for fifty years, meant that the barrel could easily have exploded and took my head off with it!

The shot gun, Meg and me became inseparable. The meadows and moorlands of the area became our very own hunting grounds, with some of the farmers giving me cartridges to shoot rabbits on their land. Whatever I shot, I'd skin and cook for Meg and me to eat that night.

On a couple of occasions I was really lucky and, as well as me shooting a rabbit, Meg also caught a live one. The first time it happened, I was amazed, not that Meg had caught a rabbit, because I knew how fast she was, but that she managed to catch it and bring it to me in her mouth without harming it. On those occasions I'd take both rabbits home, skin and cook the one I'd shot and tie some string around one of the live rabbit's legs, tying the other end of the string to the kitchen table. You see, we didn't have fridges in those days, so I had to keep the rabbit alive until Meg and me needed it, so that it stayed fresh!

For a while pickings were good and I even started to believe that I would never be hungry again.

I hadn't taken into account that it was still summer and that finding animals to shoot for food in winter would be a lot more difficult, as in winter everything went to ground.

25
A CASE OF FOWL PLAY

By the end of Spring, 1953, when I was thirteen, Dad had been in hospital for over a year.

I still visited him as often as I could, riding over Cowling Moss on my tandem, but it was very upsetting seeing how unwell and so unlike himself that Dad was.

Dad had lost so much weight and, with each visit that I made, I'd notice that he was even thinner than the last time. What made it even worse was the fact that he still hadn't regained his ability to speak. Every visit, I'd sit by the side of Dad's bed and he would get hold of my hand and try to speak to me. I know that there was something that he felt was important, that he was desperate to tell me, but, try as he might, he couldn't form and say any words. I could see the sheer frustration on his face, as he strived to rediscover his voice and make himself heard. His eyes would be fixed on mine and they spoke loud and clear about how frustrated he was. Ultimately, on each visit, his frustration would overcome him and he'd start to cry.

To see my big, strong, fearless Dad, lying there shrinking before my eyes and reduced to sobs of frustration, broke my heart and I felt helpless because I knew inside that, whatever it was that Dad was so determined to tell me, I would never hear him say it.

With Dad crying, a nurse would always come over, put her arm around my shoulder, and tell me that Dad needed to rest and it was best that I leave. I always felt lost and upset when I left Dad, but on that particular day, when Dad had been in hospital for a little over a year, as I left I knew that Dad was never going to come home. Feeling hopelessly lost, forlorn and desperately alone, I rode back over the Moss, asking 'Why?' over and over. Why had our Mam had to die and why were we going to lose our Dad?

It had started to rain just as I left the hospital, so by the time I got back to Pondhill after riding the thirteen miles over the misty Cowling Moss road, I was tired and sodden to the skin. Even though I was feeling really low, the sight of Meg coming bounding out of the farm to greet me made me feel better.

Madge was at home and she had a good fire burning in the range.

"Take your wet clothes off," she said, as she gave me a blanket to wrap around me. Once I was wrapped in the blanket and sat in front of the fire, Madge asked how Dad was.

"Just the same," I told her, "And I know he's not going to get better, so don't try telling me 'owt different!"

"Don't be silly, of course he's going to get better," Madge said, trying to cheer me up. No matter what she said, or how many times she said it, I didn't believe her, because, in my heart, I could feel the fact that he would never come back to the farm.

With there only being me and Madge at home, and Madge herself being only 16, there was nobody to reassure me and make me believe that everything would be alright. Left with all these thoughts running unchecked through my head, I often took myself off across the moors. I loved walking round the moors with Meg and my gun, it was so peaceful and I would be lost in a world of my own.

During the spring, I would sometimes find a nest of tewit (lapwing) eggs, which I'd take home and boil. They were delicious. I remember one summer morning, Meg was licking my face wanting me to get out of bed. If I tried to push her away, she thought I was playing, so, in the end she won and I got up. As I was dressing, I looked out of the bedroom window into the meadow and saw what I thought was a clutch of game birds, feeding on fallen grass seeds.

"That's our dinner for tonight, Meg!" I said aloud, as I scrambled to finish getting dressed, raced downstairs and grabbed my shotgun. With Meg hot on my heels, quickly and quietly I raced through the kitchen door and across to the wall. I peeped over the garden wall and could hardly believe my luck - the birds were still feeding. I took aim and pulled my trigger, grinning all over my face as I saw that I'd got two of the birds with one shot. I was so excited, two birds for dinner, how lucky was that!

As soon as I'd taken my shot, Meg, in a flash, raced into the field, picked up the dead birds and brought them to me. I looked at the birds lying in front of me, but didn't know what type of bird they were.

"Let's go and show them to Ken, he'll know what breed the birds are, Meg." I announced, scooping up the birds and setting off with Meg at my heel.

Ken took one look at the birds and a frown appeared on his face.

"By 'eck, Joe, you'll be in reet trouble. Them birds are guinea-fowl and they belong to Big Norman." Ken said that the best thing that I could do would be to pluck them as quickly as I could, hide the feathers in his muck midden, and cover them over with the muck.

I've never plucked a bird so fast in my life and, whilst my hands were plucking away, my eyes kept darting around, watching out for any sign of Big Norman - I didn't want his huge clog coming into contact with my backside!

Having finished the plucking and buried the evidence, I raced back to Pondhill. I put the birds into a big stew pot, with onions and potatoes and placed it on the range in the kitchen. I smiled down at Meg, who was sat watching me - tonight we would fill our bellies.

All of a sudden, the door opened and young Norman was there. He'd come down to Pondhill to ask if I would help him to look for his dad's guinea-fowls. He told me that his father would kick his backside if he didn't find them, as young Norman had been told to fasten the door to the guinea-fowl hut the night before, but he'd forgot and the birds had got out.

I hoped he couldn't smell the guinea-fowls cooking on the range and wanted to get him out of the kitchen as soon as possible, so I told him that of course I'd help him, adding that the quicker we started looking the better, as I pushed him back out of the door.

We started looking in the fields and, after about half hour, Norman spotted four of his guinea-fowls. "Oh 'eck," he said, "we had six."

"Maybe the fox got two of them." I said with as much conviction as I could muster.

"Aye, Joe, tha' could be reet." Norman agreed with me, making me feel more guilty than ever.

As guilty as I felt, I had to make sure that Norman didn't want to put off going home to face the music by stopping off at Pondhill on the way, so, scarcely able to look him in the eye, I continued, "You're lucky the fox didn't kill them all, Norman. Let's get these four back to yours as quick as we can, before fox comes back again."

We got the four remaining fowls back to the hut and Norman fastened the door securely. Thanking me again for my help, he then turned and, dragging his feet, made his way back to the farmhouse, to tell his father why they now only had four guinea fowl.

At that point I said a very quick goodbye and me and Meg ran back to Pondhill. I was feeling horribly guilty, but, at the same time, my belly was rumbling at the thought of the feast it was about to enjoy.

I'm not sure that I ever did tell Norman that it was me and Meg and not the fox who had his dad's guinea fowl. So Norman, if you're reading this and I haven't told you before, can I just say that I'm sorry if your father kicked your backside, but if it's any consolation me and Meg thought the guinea fowl were delicious.

26
WE LOSE OUR DAD – PONDHILL IS AT RISK

When John's car pulled up outside Pondhill, before either Madge had left for work, or I had left for school, I knew it could only mean still more sad news.

Ada and John got out of the car, came into the farmhouse, and told us that Dad had passed away during the night.

My first thought was that Madge and me are orphans now. Even when Dad was in hospital, he was still with us, but now we had no one. I felt sad about Dad, but not the terrible grief that I had felt when Mam had died.

With Dad having been in hospital for two years, we had got used to him not being at the farm and, as I've previously said, for the second year that he was away, something inside me knew that he was never coming home. That said, on hearing the news, both Madge and I felt an emptiness and the kitchen felt suddenly cold.

Dad was brought back to the farm from the hospital and his coffin was put in the front parlour. There weren't Chapels Of Rest in those days and it was traditional for the deceased to be brought home until the funeral. I wasn't frightened by Dad's coffin being in the house, but when I went to bed I cuddled up close to Meg and pulled the bed covers over my head.

Over the next few days, farmers, neighbours and relatives called at the farm, to pay their respects and to tell us how sorry they were about our loss. When I saw the first group of relatives arriving, I quickly pulled Madge to one side and told her that, no matter what any relative said, I was going to Dad's funeral.

We arranged Dad's funeral, but whereas after Mam's funeral folk came back for tea and sandwiches, this time Madge and me had no money to spend on a tea. We told everyone that visited about the funeral arrangements and could see that some of them were disappointed that everyone wasn't returning to Pondhill after the service. That's when I first learned that some folk only go to funerals for the feed that they get afterwards.

Once again the gleaming black hearse left Pondhill, this time carrying Dad's coffin to be buried with Mam at Cock Hill Cemetery. To save on the cost, Madge and I went in John and Ada's car. Madge was upset and I tried my best to comfort her in the car as we drove to the church. After the service, we arrived at the windswept, bleak graveyard at Cock Hill and that is when it hit me. All of I sudden I again felt that terrible loneliness and ache in my stomach.

Standing at the grave side, I watched, helpless, as Dad's coffin was lowered into the ground. All that I could see was this dark hole in the ground, where, two years earlier, Mam had been laid to rest. I don't remember much else about the funeral, I was too upset and just wanted to wake up in my bed at Pondhill and find that it was all a bad dream.

Back home after the funeral, Ada and John said they would get in touch with the solicitor, to let him know that Dad had died. I didn't know why we had to tell him, but Ada said that it was the law. I left them talking in the house and Meg and me went and sat on Cuckoo Rock, listening to the birds. I sat there, remembering how, when I was small, my Dad would bring me up on to the rock, where we would sit together and he would point out the names and sounds of the different birds and how we would play a game where he would point out birds flying above us and I had to guess what they were. I started to realise just how much I missed my parents.

At least I had Meg and Madge and I had each other. I think I was saying it to convince myself, but, sitting there on Cuckoo Rock, I told

Meg that as long as we had each other and Pondhill, we would some-how be alright.

However, within a few short weeks of Dad's funeral, more devastating news arrived.

We never got any mail at Pondhill, so I was surprised when I looked out one Saturday morning and saw the postman coming down the lane. I went outside and met him part way up the lane.

"Morning young Joe, this looks like an important letter for you." the postman said as he gave the envelope to me. Thanking him, I turned and ran back to the farm, where I burst into the kitchen, shouting.

"Madge, Madge, we've just had a letter delivered."

Madge came into the kitchen, opened the letter and started to read it aloud. As she read it she went very pale and started to cry. For all that she'd read the letter out loud, I didn't understand what it meant, but the look on Madge's face and the tears running down her cheeks started the all too familiar feeling in my stomach that told me that it was bad news.

"What's up Madge? What's it about?" I managed to ask.

"It's bad news," she sobbed, "we have to leave Pondhill."

"But we can't," I said, struggling to take in what she had said. As we both stood, shocked into silence, all I could think was that not only are we orphans, but now we are going to be homeless too.

Poor Madge, she was barely sixteen and already had the responsibility of looking after me as well as herself. Now it looked like she would also have to find a place for us to live.

It turned out that, because Mam and Dad had never married, their offspring, namely me and Madge, were not entitled to inherit Pondhill from them.

Under the law, the farm would go to Dad's brother, our Uncle John-ny.

I wouldn't say I knew him well, but Uncle Johnny had been to Pondhill on a number of occasions. I'd seen him at Dad's funeral and remembered thinking how he was the same build as Dad had been before he became ill and that he looked like I remembered Dad once looked. Anyone that saw them would know that they were brothers. Now, he was going to inherit Pondhill, our home, and make us homeless.

We sat there for ages, trying to make some sort of sense out of the horrible news that we'd received. All sorts of thoughts were going through my head, as I tried to take in the news and wondered what the future held for us now.

"Maybe we can rent the farm from Uncle Johnny," I eventually said, looking hopefully at Madge.

"I don't think we'll be able to," Madge said, "I think he will sell it."

"He can't sell it!" I spluttered, tears stinging my eyes, "where will we go? I'm not going in a boys' home, I'll run away first!"

"Don't be silly, Joe, I'll think of something." Madge tried to reassure me, but I knew that she was as much at a loss over what we could do as I was.

Later that same morning, Clive came over and I told him what had happened.

"Oh heck, Joe, that's awful, but don't worry, you can come and live with us, I know my Mam wouldn't mind."

"But what about Meg?" I said.

"She can come too, I like Meg."

Clive was adamant, but their house was only a small cottage and I didn't think his Mam would want a dog, no matter how sure Clive sounded.

That Saturday night, me and Meg went to bed, but I couldn't sleep. I tossed and turned all night long, asking questions inside my head. 'How could this have happened?' 'Where could we go?' 'How could we have lost everything that Mam and Dad had worked for?"

I wearily made my way downstairs on Sunday morning, to find that Madge was already up and had lit the fire. I told Madge that I hadn't been able to sleep all night and she admitted that she too had had a restless night of no sleep.

Neither of us wanted anything to eat, so we sat with a pot of tea, in front of the range, just looking into the fire. Finally, I could hold it in no longer and, with eyes leaking once more, I turned to face Madge.

"Why has this happened to us, Madge?"

She didn't say anything, but turned to me and gave me a hug, her eyes full of tears too.

Later in the morning, I called Meg and we walked round the fields, before finding ourselves down at Tinkle Beck. I stood there, thinking of the times I had played in the beck with Clive, Maurice and Norman and allowed myself a sad smile as I remembered the day that Mam had fetched a pair of Madge's silk knickers for me to use as trunks. I reckoned that soon enough someone else would be making their memories, playing in the beck. As me and Meg started walking back towards Pondhill, I wondered if I'd ever know such fun times again.

When we got back to the farm, Madge had made a sandwich, but I didn't want anything to eat. I think that we were both in a state of shock, with neither of us able to believe, never mind understand, what was happening.

Suddenly, Meg started to growl under her breath. I went to look through the kitchen window and saw that someone was walking down the lane to the farm. As I realised who it was, I got that same ache in my stomach that was visiting me far too often.

"Oh, Madge, it's Uncle Johnny. He's come to turn us out."

I was on the verge of tears again, as I told my sister who it was.

Neither of our frightened faces held the slightest bit of colour, as we just stood there dreading the knock on the door that we knew was coming. Although we were waiting for it, when the knock came we both jumped and our hearts started beating faster and louder than ever before.

Somehow, I managed to make my feet move and I stepped over to the door, opened it and heard a voice that sounded a little bit like mine inviting Uncle Johnny to come in.

As Uncle Johnny moved into the kitchen Madge asked if he'd like to sit down and have a pot of tea. Uncle Johnny thanked her and sat down, then, without wasting another second, he came straight to the point of his visit.

"Did you receive your letter from the solicitor yesterday?" Johnny looked at Madge and then me as he spoke.

"Yes" we both croaked a reply.

"Well, so did I and I thought I should come over and sort it out straight away" Uncle Johnny told us.

He looked at Madge, then me again before he continued, holding our gaze as he spoke.

"I've got no intention of taking your inheritance. This farm belongs to you two, because that's what your Dad would have wanted. I'm going to see my solicitor tomorrow to make sure that whatever bits of paper get sorted so that the farm is yours."

Madge and me could not believe what we were hearing and were thanking him, crying and hugging each other, all at the same time.

When we'd calmed down a little bit, Uncle Johnny carried on talking. His face showed genuine concern when he asked whether we could manage here on our own, Pondhill being so far out of the village and us being so young.

We managed to refrain from pointing out that we'd been living there on our own for the last two years, as we both said that we were sure we could manage.

Uncle Johnny still didn't look convinced.

"Well, if you need any help you must get in touch with me. You're very young to be living here by yourselves."

Madge told him that she was earning good money at the mill and that we would be able to manage.

With that, and having finished his tea, Uncle Johnny got up, said his goodbyes and, after again promising to go straight to the solicitors in the morning, left.

Madge and I looked at each other then, as the tears started again, hugged. For once, our tears were tears of joy.

I have never forgotten what Uncle Johnny did for us. He would have been well within his rights to take the farm and either kick us out, or to take the farm but let us stay there until we'd grown up and then kick us out so that he could sell it. I might not have known him too well, but, his making sure that legal title for the farm was signed over to Madge and I, because he knew it was what Dad would have wanted, tells me everything about the decency and honesty of the man.

27
JOYRIDING – 1950's STYLE

One day, while I was walking home from school, I saw some men working in the valley just below our farm. I climbed onto the top of the wall to get a better view and see what they were doing. I could see a few Jeeps, which made me think that the men were Yanks, but I couldn't work out why the Yanks would be in Cowling.

Still puzzling over it as I walked back up the lane, I bumped into Norman, who was coming the other way, down the lane. I was sure that Norman would know what was going on.

"Norman, what's them Yanks doing in valley?" I asked.

"Up to no good" came his assured reply.

"I knew it!" I said. "What are they up to then?" I pressed him, wanting all the details.

"I don't know. Me father just said that they were bound to be up to no good."

Norman shrugged as he confirmed that he knew as little about the men and Jeeps as I did.

By the time I'd got home and Meg had excitedly greeted me, the Yanks with Jeeps had slipped to the back of my mind. The next morning, Saturday, Clive came over to Pondhill. As soon as he arrived he asked what the Jeeps were doing in the valley.

"By 'eck, I'd forgotten about them" I said. I told him that they'd been there the day before and that Big Norman had said that they were up to no good. We looked at each other and an unspoken 'what are we waiting for' passed between us, as we ran out of Pondhill, with Meg in tow, on a mission to find out what the Yanks were doing in our valley.

We climbed on top of the wall to get a good view down across the fields and were rewarded by seeing that, whilst all the men had gone, the Jeeps were still there. Without wasting another second, we scrambled down from the wall and ran over the fields to where three Jeeps were parked. As we slid to a halt by the jeeps, Meg, who hadn't been able to get up on top of the wall, came running up. She must have ran along to the gate and found a way through it.

We started exploring the Jeeps and couldn't believe our luck – the ignition keys had been left in one of them. That was just too much temptation for two young lads.

"Let's see if we can start it up." I said to Clive, as I jumped into the driver's seat.

Clive got in the front, next to me, and Meg jumped into the back.

"Do you know how to drive one of these?" Clive asked, knowing that it wouldn't make any difference even if I couldn't.

I didn't have a clue how to drive and that's what I meant when I answered him.

"Well, sort of."

I turned the key and the Jeep thundered into life and lurched forward about two foot before stopping, nearly throwing Clive and Meg out in the process!

Undeterred, I started it up again and, once more, we were all thrown forward, before the Jeep stopped once more.

After a few more tries, and with my passengers well shaken, I got the hang of it and we were off.

We drove around the field, down into the valley, and then back up again, Clive and myself taking it in turn to drive.

I call it a field, but that doesn't begin to describe it. The ground was very uneven, rising and falling unpredictably, with a generous number of big stones and boulders, many of which were hidden by vegetation, randomly sited over the whole area. Just for good measure, the whole thing was on a steep incline, bringing the hills down to meet the valley floor. Hopefully you get the picture.

Hardly surprising then that the Jeep was bouncing around all over the place. Several times it came close to turning over completely, but our excitement far outweighed any fear that we may have had and we were laughing and shouting encouragement to each other as we careered around the field. We both took turns at driving, seeing who dare go the fastest.

The excitement that we felt must have been intoxicating, because we threw that Jeep around the field for an hour, without once thinking that what we were doing was dangerous.

All of a sudden the Jeep came to a stop. It had run out of fuel. We were about to accept that our new game was over, when Meg started barking from the back of the Jeep. As we looked to see what was causing her to bark, we saw that she was standing next to a jerry can full of fuel. Our excitement levels raised again, Clive and I added our whoops of delight to Meg's barking.

There was only one small problem – neither of us knew how to fill the fuel tank and, try as we might, we couldn't work it out.

"My Dad will know, he was in the army." Clive announced.

We decided that we'd go and ask Clive's Dad and were just thinking of how we could ask him without telling him why, when we heard a loud, booming voice from beyond the field.

We looked round and saw my neighbour, Ken, making his way into our field and realised that the angry noise coming out of his mouth was aimed at us.

"What the heck do you think you're doing? You could have broken your necks driving around the field like that!"

We thought about legging it, but I had seen Ken running around his field after his animals and I knew he would catch us. With Dad in hospital, Ken had kept an eye on me and, when I deserved it, had given me a clip round the ear. So I knew that if we ran and made Ken catch us, then he might give us a good hiding. So, heads down, we walked slowly towards him, to face the music.

"Sorry, Ken."

Well, what else could we say?

Eyes fixed firmly on the ground, I was listening for the swoosh of air that meant that an arm was swinging towards me and my head was about to hurt. A few seconds passed and then, instead of a swoosh, we heard Ken's voice.

"You young buggers get off home, now."

We didn't need telling twice.

In adult life, I've returned and looked at that field where we had our first experience of driving. It left me wondering how we hadn't killed ourselves that day. The truth is, I wouldn't drive round that field in a Jeep now, as an experienced driver, I think even Evil Knievel would have thought twice about it. I'm just glad we didn't know how to fill the Jeep up with fuel, our luck surely wouldn't have held out if we'd had another tank's worth of driving at breakneck speed around it. .

As an aside, we later found out that the Yanks had been investigating the possibility of building a dam in the valley.

As we made our way back to Pondhill, relieved to have escaped with nothing more than being shouted at, Clive reminded me that the following Saturday was the day of the local gala. This was always a big day in the village and, as part of the festivities, there was always a fancy dress competition. Clive suggested that we should enter the competition.

"There's no way I'm going to gala in fancy dress!" I quickly told him, letting the tone of my voice convey my disgust at the idea.

"First prize is 2/6 (two and six)." Clive replied.

Now, two shillings and sixpence, or 2/6, was a lot of money for two young lads and I quickly forgot about how disgusted I was at the idea of being seen in fancy dress.

"What can we go as?" I said. "I've only got the clothes I'm standing in, never mind any fancy dress."

"Let's see if your Ada has any ideas" Clive suggested.

So we spoke to Ada and she did have an idea, which somehow they persuaded me to go along with.

So it was that, the following Saturday, 'Daisy Daisy' was one of the entrants in the fancy dress competition.

'Daisy Daisy' featured my tandem, with a grinning Clive dressed in striped pyjamas and a boater hat and me, feeling daft, wearing one of Ada's blouses, one of Ada's skirts and with a bonnet on my head!

It's amazing what the thought of two and six can make someone do!

When the judges stood to announce the decision, me and Clive, for once, were totally silent. As we heard the words 'and the winner is - Daisy Daisy', Clive leapt up into the air and I threw off the bonnet, skirt and blouse!

The two and six in our pockets, we were off – straight to the shop to buy some cigarettes.

28
The Kid Hunter, Cigarettes and Girls

Once Madge and I knew that the farm belonged to us and that we could stay there without fear of anyone turning us off it, we were really pleased and settled into a routine that suited us.

For Madge, that routine involved going to work. As for me, well, since Dad died I preferred wandering around the moors with Meg and my gun for company rather than going to school, so that's what I did.

Now, let me tell you, given all the troubles that we'd faced, you'd think we'd have learnt by then, that whenever we thought things were running smoothly, that's exactly when trouble would rear its head again.

We hadn't.

Not only had we not learnt to expect trouble, but by staying away from school I was actually inviting it to pay us a visit and, sure enough, it did.

Back then, if a child was away from school for more than a week or so, without a note having been sent to school to explain the absence, the school would involve the school inspector, better known by one and all as the Kid Hunter.

Sure enough, as I was off roaming the moors, the Kid Hunter had come looking for me. Not finding me at Pondhill, he nosed around until he found Ada. Ada didn't waste any time in putting him right, insisting that his information was wrong, she knew for a fact that I had definitely been at school, because she'd seen Clive and me at the bus stop. The more the poor man tried to point out my prolonged absence, the more Ada sprang to my defence and reiterated her certain knowledge that I had been going to school.

You can imagine how furious she was when, later that day, after listening to her tale about the Kid Hunter and how she'd sent him packing with a flea in his ear, I had to confess that me and Clive may have waited at the bus stop, but when we saw the bus coming we jumped over the wall and hid until the bus went past.

Suffice to say, after my confession, Ada told me in no uncertain terms exactly what she would do to me, if I didn't go to school, which, I was left in no doubt, would be a lot worse than anything the Kid Hunter could inflict.

When I got to school the next day, Andrew asked me where I'd been. Before I had a chance to speak, one of the other boys, Peter, jumped in, saying that he bet I'd been trailing around the moors with my gun and dog. If they'd looked at my face right then, they would have known that he had got it spot on, but just then the bell rang, so I put my head down, laughed and headed for the classroom. As I went in, I handed a note to the waiting teacher. Hurriedly scrawled by Ada, it told all about the really bad dose of flu that I'd had.

Having decided that going to school would be good for my health, I quickly got myself back into all the activities I'd previously done. So, as soon as play time started, along with Andrew, Peter and Clive, I headed straight behind the bike shed for a cigarette. I say for a cigarette, but in truth it was usually the case that, between us, there would be one cigarette, which would be passed around the four of us, rapidly having the life sucked out of it.

For all there was often only one measly fag to share, us boys enjoyed our play time and lunch time smoke. Obviously, as we were smoking, we all felt grown up, but there was also the added excitement of the danger of being caught at any time by a teacher. Even more than this though, we would often be joined by a few of the lasses, who would demand that we share the cig with them, or they'd tell the teacher. Us boys would all moan to each other about the girls coming round and making us share our cigs, but, not that any of us would ever admit it, secretly we all liked them and enjoyed showing off, acting big in front of them.

Normally, more because of a lack of cigarettes than any other reason, my cigarette smoking was confined to the school bike shed, or in 'Sawbinjack', the gang hut. One summer evening though, when it was just on the edge of dark, Meg and me were sauntering back from the village when I heard voices coming from the village War Memorial shelter. We didn't have such things as coffee bars then, so the shelter was a place where a lot of the teenagers would hang out, even though it was in a field in front of the grave yard!

That evening, when I looked, I found that the voices were from some lads and lasses who I knew, but who were older than me.

"Is that you, Joe?" one shouted.

"Aye, I'm on me way home." I shouted back.

"Come in and have a cig if you want."

Well, I didn't need telling twice, after all, I was being asked to join the older kids.

Feeling well happy, I went straight into the shelter. I wasn't even that disappointed when all that they gave me was a tab end, I was just happy to be involved, hanging out with the older kids, all of us acting the goat and having a laugh.

After a while, some of the lads stopped joking around and started cuddling and kissing the lasses. I'm sure I was staring, but nobody said anything. They were too busy concentrating on what they were doing and anyway, it was getting dark in there, so they probably wouldn't have been able to notice that I was watching them.

Next thing I knew, one of the lasses started cuddling me, then, without warning, she gave me a kiss.

"This is alreet!" I thought, quickly recovering from the shock of my first kiss.

I was disappointed when I felt her arms letting me go, but she was only reaching for a cig.

"Do you want a cig, Joe?" she asked as she offered one to me.

I took it and put it between my lips, leaning slightly forward as she struck the match.

I should have known it couldn't last!

As the match flared and I leant forward, she got a look at my face.

"How old are you?" she gasped.

"Sixteen", I lied.

"He's only thirteen", one of the other boys laughingly said from somewhere in the shelter.

"I'm nearly fourteen!" I heard myself saying loudly in defence of the sudden challenge.

The slap across my face was so loud that, for a second, I couldn't hear them all laughing.

My cheek might have been red and stinging, but I had a big smile on my face as me and Meg set off again for Pondhill. I'd been kissed by a lass for the first time and I felt great.

I couldn't wait to tell Clive the next morning that I'd been kissing lasses, he'd be dead jealous.

All the way home I replayed the kiss over and over in my head. I was so proud of myself and didn't mind that she wasn't the best looking of lasses. The way I looked at it, it was a start!

29
MADGE ATTRACTS ATTENTION

Madge was growing up into a nice looking lass and I knew the lads were interested in her. I think Norman was a bit sweet on her, as he was always asking me how she was!

One evening, as Madge got herself ready to go out, she put lipstick on and coloured her cheeks with something called rouge. I thought it looked daft and told her so, but she said that all the girls were putting it on their cheeks.

Satisfied with her handy-work, off she went, waving and saying she wouldn't be late home. I'd heard that before, but I told myself that I didn't mind.

"Come on Meg, let's finish the rabbit stew off. I think there's plenty for a plate each." I said, looking down at my dog. She trotted towards me across the kitchen, and then waited patiently while I shared the stew between us.

She might have waited while I shared it out, but as soon as I put her dish on the floor her head was into it and, within two seconds, she was licking the dish clean.

"By gum Meg, tha's guzzled that down quick." I told her, as she sat watching me eat mine, waiting in hope for me to drop some.

Not having much to do, and knowing that Madge would be late home, I decided that I'd go and torment Ken, so, leaving Meg in the kitchen, I ran down the field to Ken's farm.

Edna, seeing me coming, had the kitchen door open. As I went into their kitchen, Ken, sat at the table, turned to face me.

"What do you want, you young bugger?" he laughingly said.

"Nowt particular, I just thought I'd come and torment you," I cheekily told him.

With that, Ken was out of his chair and lunging for me. Grabbing hold of me, we started having one of our regular wrestling matches. Sometimes he would let me win, but other times Ken made sure that he won.

I don't know how Edna put up with us wrestling all around the kitchen floor, even if it was a very big farm house kitchen. Almost inevitably, we would end up sending the table and chairs flying, then Edna's patience would run out and she'd tell us to stop, complaining that Ken was acting like a big kid and should have more sense and warning us that she didn't want the bairns wakening up.

*

I loved going down to Ken and Edna's. They were like family to me and the kitchen reminded me of when Mam was alive, always filled with the smell of baking and cooking.

One night, just as it was coming dark and I had just lit the candles in the kitchen, Madge was doing some ironing, when we heard a knock on the door. We both looked at each other and Meg growled, all three of us wondering who could be at the door, as we never got any visitors.

I went to the door and asked who was there.

"It's Fred, I work with your Madge," came the reply, so I let him in.

He was medium height, a bit scruffy and he wore the smell of the mill. I took an instant dislike to this chap and, looking at our Madge, I could tell that she didn't think much about him either, which begged the question, what did he want?

"I just called to see how you are both getting on," he said, as, uninvited, he plonked himself down on the sofa.

"We are both alreet," I said, looking over at Madge, who had just finished her ironing.

"Are you going to make me a pot of tea, Madge? It's a long walk from the village."

Our unwanted visitor was making himself comfortable.

"We can't," I said, "we have just run out of tea."

Madge looked at me with her eyes nearly popping out of her head, but she did agree with me and said how sorry she was that she could not make him a pot of tea. Fred wasn't going to be put off so easily.

"Come and sit on the sofa Madge, you look tired." he said, as he patted the seat next to him.

Madge, unsure what to do, hesitated, so Fred continued.

"Don't be frightened, I'm not going to bite."

Madge reluctantly went and sat on the edge of the sofa. We both felt very vulnerable, faced with his over-confident, almost aggressive behaviour and didn't know what we should do.

Fortunately, Meg sensed our discomfort, jumped up and stood facing Fred, making a very deep, loud growling sound. She was an angry dog.

"I don't think my dog likes you," I said, as Meg increased the volume of her growling.

"No and I don't like dogs," Fred said, as he cautiously stood, before making a dash for the door.

As soon as he was through it, I shut and locked the door. I turned to Madge and smiled, telling her I didn't think we would see him again. How wrong I was.

A few days later, Fred returned, but this time he didn't knock on the door, he just walked straight in, causing both me and Madge to jump in shock.

"I brought you a packet of tea," he said, before adding with a smirk on his face, "now you can make me a pot of tea."

This time I was angry. How dare he walk straight into the kitchen. I whispered, so as not to be overheard, telling Madge that I would go for Ken.

Leaving Meg to look after Madge, I ran, as fast as my legs would carry me, over the fields to Ken's farm. They heard me shouting for them as I approached and were in the doorway as I raced up to the door.

"What on earth is the matter, Joe?" both Ken and Edna said together.

"It's that Fred, he's back again."

I had hardly got the words out of my mouth, when Ken was out of the kitchen door and racing across the fields to Pondhill, with a face like thunder.

Arriving at the farm, Ken burst into the kitchen and grabbed Fred by the scruff of the neck. As he then threw him out of the kitchen door, Ken let him know that if he ever came back Ken would happily break his neck.

Having sprinted home, trying to catch up with Ken, I'd arrived just in time to see all the action. I couldn't help but show my excitement to my new hero.

"By 'eck Ken, you told him. I bet he nearly peed 'is pants when you burst into the kitchen!"

Before Ken left, he asked us if we were both okay and told us not to worry, as he didn't think that bugger would trouble us again.

Ken was right, that was the last we ever saw of Fred.

30
SHOPPING ON THE MOORS & FOUR GO CAMPING

When we started going onto the moors, it didn't take either me or Meg long to understand the rules, which were really very simple – generally speaking. If we didn't shoot or catch anything, then we didn't eat.

The moors were like our local shop and my gun was the money that I used to get our food.

One bright summer day, we had been walking for what seemed like hours across the moor, without so much as a sniff at a shot, when we reached the stone building which was used as the shooting hut.

It had been built in 1902 for the early shooters who used the moor and later generations of shooters had seen no reason not to continue using it.

The door was open, so, poking my head through it, I shouted out a hello and ventured inside. All the walking had made me feel tired and this feeling was exaggerated by me feeling down about the complete lack of luck we'd had in finding anything to have a shot at.

I decided that I needed a rest, so sat on an old wooden chair. Meg, panting heavily, lay down on the flagstone floor. I knew that both Meg and I needed a drink, so I started looking about inside the hut. I spotted a beer crate full of bottles, obviously left by the shooters, so went over and got one out.

The label said Guinness. I took the cap off by striking it on the top rail of the chair and took a swig of the frothy liquid. Just as quickly as I had took the drink, so I spat it out! I did not like the taste of Guinness.

Meg was looking at me, still panting heavily. I found an old tin dish and poured a bottle of the Guinness into the dish and gave it to her. She obviously liked it more than I did, because she swigged down the contents of the dish in a flash, then looked up at me and licked her lips. I watched her, amused, because it looked like she was 'doggy - laughing' and was wagging her tail non-stop.

After we'd rested for a while, we left the stone hut and I watched Meg as she padded away across the rough moorland in the general direction of Pondhill, but not keeping a very straight line. It then dawned on me that the bottle of Guinness Meg had so eagerly lapped up had made her a bit drunk. On we went, Meg weaving occasionally and me, walking behind, grinning.

As we were finally nearing home and still not having had a shot at anything, I was beginning to think we were going to have a night without eating. Having all but given up, I was too slow with the gun when a bit of luck did come our way.

Just as we were passing the empty hen hut, a rabbit suddenly ran out from beneath it. As I said, I wasn't ready with the gun and the rabbit took off hopping for its life down the meadow. Quick as a flash, Meg, drunk or not, raced like quicksilver down the meadow after the rabbit and caught the terrified creature in her mouth. She then turned and ran back to where I was stood watching and dropped it at my feet.

"Good lass Meg!" I shouted happily, as I picked up the rabbit and we finished our journey home, where I soon had the rabbit skinned and in the cooking pot.

That night me and Meg ate well and Meg in particular slept soundly.

Back at school, our teacher said that us boys could do with an adventure and suggested that we go camping one weekend, and then tell the class all about it when we got back.

Me wanting an adventure - he obviously didn't have a clue how I lived! Nevertheless, Clive, Andrew, Peter and me said that we would do it.

So it was arranged that we would go the following Saturday.

It would mean that I had to leave Meg with Madge, so I gave Madge instructions on what she had to do and told her to let Meg sleep on my bed.

Saturday morning arrived. We'd agreed that I would take bread and beans; Clive would take water and matches; Andrew, whose Mam was a good baker, would bring some buns; and Peter would bring the tent.

We'd decided to catch the bus from Crosshill to Skipton, a bus ride of about four miles, then take a bus to Gargrave, this being about five more miles. That was the plan.

None of us had been to Gargrave before and, not long after getting on the second bus, we panicked, worried that if we went all the way to Gargrave we'd get lost, and so we decided to get off the bus then, two miles outside of Skipton.

Having left the bus, we scouted around for a camp site, finally settling on a farmer's field where, full of enthusiasm, we started to put up the tent. Two hours later, we at last managed to get the tent to stand up. The next job was to light a camp fire, which was easy enough and we soon had it blazing away. In fact, the flames were so impressive that it made me think it was a little bit too close to the tent. I pointed this out to the others, but Peter said it would be okay.

Safety worries over, we carried on.

With the fire blazing nicely, our thoughts turned to our bellies, with all of us suddenly realising that we were getting hungry. This was of course no problem to such a well prepared team as us, as all I had to do was get a tin of beans out of my bag.

"Did anyone bring a tin opener?" I asked, realising that we'd hit a slight snag.

As you've guessed, none of us had thought to bring a tin opener, but

158

such a small setback wasn't going to deter me.

"Don't worry," I announced, "I'll bash it open with a stone."

After hitting it with a stone for about ten minutes, the tin can was squashed, but still not open.

Suddenly we weren't hungry, we were starving!

At that point, you might have expected our enthusiasm to drop and normally you'd be right, but Andrew came up with the right thing to say, just at the right time.

"Not to worry, everyone, Joe can catch a rabbit for our tea."

Instantly, everyone felt better and that feeling that all was well with the world lasted for a good ten seconds, until I spoke.

"Not without a gun I can't."

Of course, we were all in danger of dying of starvation by then and, gun or no gun, I had to get us a rabbit, or we faced certain death, miles from home!

As panic started to set in around me, I knew I had to stay calm and come up with a plan.

"Right, this is what we'll do," I said confidently. "We'll stand by a rabbit hole and, when one pops out, we'll grab it!"

Now, as you'd expect with such a fool-proof plan, smiling faces were the order of the day again and, with everyone sure that certain death by starvation had been avoided, we started looking for rabbit holes.

Finding rabbit holes was easy, there were loads of them. There was just one small problem, the fact that rabbits aren't stupid enough to come out of their holes when a group of lads are standing by them!

Doubts about my great plan were starting to be voiced and I knew that something had to happen quickly to stop everyone from thinking about how hungry they were.

What happened next certainly did that.

"Blinking 'eck!" Clive yelled, "The tent's on fire!"

Rabbits and empty bellies were the furthest things from our minds as we ran back to the tent.

When we got there, all we could do was watch in shock and amazement as the flames, which were everywhere, ate the tent, until it was no more.

We were all in shock, but Peter, in particular, had gone white. It turned out that he'd borrowed the tent from a lad at school, who happened to be a very big lad.

"He's gonna bash my head in," Peter said with terror in his voice.

"I'm glad I didn't borrow it from him." Andrew's words did little to make Peter feel any better.

Tired, hungry and defeated we picked up what was left of our things and went to catch the bus home, all of us worrying about what we could tell the class on Monday, except Peter, who couldn't have cared less about the embarrassment that telling our story would heap upon us and would gladly have taken that in place of the beating that he knew was coming to him.

All the way home on the bus we argued about what we should tell the class on Monday. Finally, I realised that we were that hungry and tired that we'd never come up with a story that we were all in agreement with, so I told everyone to stop arguing and that I would come up with an alternative story about our camping trip for Monday morning. At least that stopped us arguing for the rest of the bus journey.

I was really feeling down as I trudged into Pondhill, but Meg came charging up to me, her tail attacking me as she jumped all over me, licking my face for all she was worth. That cheered me up a little bit.

I told Madge what had happened and, partly because she was feeling sorry for me and partly because she had no food in the house, she gave me some money to go to the chip shop. That cheered me up a little bit more.

Standing in the queue waiting, with the delicious, mouth-watering smell of freshly fried fish and chips filling the air, I started wishing that the dozen or so people in front of me would get their orders and go, instead of listening to village gossip. I was beginning to think that by the time it was my turn to be served all the fish and chips would be sold out, but, at last, I was at the front of the queue.

"Now young Joe, what's your order?"

"Fish and chips please, Mrs Gallagher."

As usual, Mrs Gallagher gave me extra chips.

That cheered me up a bit more.

As I left the chip shop, I noticed a large bundle of newspapers on the newsagent's doorstep. Meg went over to them and was only sniffing the papers when, suddenly, the door opened and the shopkeeper came out and shouted.

"Get your bloody mangy dog off my newspapers!"

"She's not a mangy dog!" I shouted back.

How dare he call Meg mangy. I tried to explain that Meg had only been sniffing the newspapers and had done no harm, but he told me to sod off and slammed the door shut.

"Come on Meg, let's go home,"

I'd turned to go but, seeing that Meg wasn't walking by my side, turned back to see where she was. Meg was still standing where she'd been when the newsagent had shouted at us. For a second she just stood and looked at me, and then she turned round, went back over to the newspapers and peed on them.

At first, I looked on in horror, but I swear Meg was laughing and I started laughing with her.

We ran back to Pondhill as fast as our legs would carry us, laughing all the way.

I was totally cheered up.

Come Monday morning and Clive was waiting for me by the bus stop.

"Have you come up with a story about the camping?" He said, by way of a greeting.

I told him that I had, but that we didn't have time to hang around while I told him, so he'd just have to wait until we were at school.

Andrew and Peter were waiting for us at the school gates and, like Clive, they greeted me with the same question.

Before I could answer them, the school bell rang out its urgent call and I walked through the school door and towards our classroom, the three others following me with a barely disguised complete lack of enthusiasm.

I wondered when the teacher would call on us to relay the details of our great adventure. I didn't have to wait long, as soon as we had finished saying our morning prayer he looked over to us and asked if one of us would step forward and tell the class about our camping experience.

I stood up and walked to the front of the class. For the first time since I'd invented the story the previous day, I had doubts as to whether the teacher and the rest of the class would believe what I was going to say.

"It's too late for second thoughts now!" I told myself.

"It's really important, when you go camping, to make sure that you take with you everything that you are likely to need." I started.

"We thought it through and made a list of everything that we needed, and then ticked off the list as we decided who was going to take what.

I pointed to the huge boy who had lent his tent to us, as I continued. "The most important piece of equipment that you need is a good tent and we were really lucky that George knew this and was kind enough to insist that we take his tent. Thank you George."

As I said thank you to him, I started clapping and all of the class quickly joined in.

I let George enjoy a few seconds of clapping before I carried on.

I explained how we had carefully packed everything on our lists and had then caught the bus to the far side of Skipton, where we soon found the ideal place to camp, in a field near to the river.

I looked around the room at the faces of my classmates and started to relax a little, as none of them were laughing and, as importantly, none of them looked like they were going to challenge anything that I was saying to them. Crikey, even Clive, Peter and Andrew looked like they believed everything that I said!

"We put the tent up in less than five minutes and soon had a camp fire burning, all ready for us to cook our tea on. Before we had our tea, though, we decided that we'd have a dip in the river, which was really refreshing."

I was in full flow now – even I was starting to believe what I was saying!

"We cooked our tea over the fire whilst we dried ourselves under the sun. What a feast we had! We ate so much that we all thought we were going to burst. It was a good job we'd gone for a dip first, because we were so full after eating our tea that all we could do was just sit down on the grass."

Everyone was still listening to my every word.

"We were going to go and sit in the tent, but, because it was so warm, we decided to just sit on the grass for a while. It's lucky that we did, or we might have died!"

Before anyone could question what I meant, I carried on.

"None of us noticed that a piece of wood had fallen off the fire and rolled across the ground to the tent, until Clive shouted that the tent was on fire!"

I could hear the gasps around the room, but, not only was I not going to be stopped now, my voice got louder as my tale raced towards its end.

"Within a few seconds the whole tent was ablaze, with flames leaping fifteen feet high. As I watched the fire devouring the canvas, all I could think about was how lucky we all were that we'd decided to sit and chat outside, otherwise we would all have burned to death!"

I let this sink in for a few seconds before telling everyone that, whilst we were still in shock, we were faced with the choice of sleeping out in the open air, or returning home. As I told them that, given what had happened, we all decided that it was best for us to pack up what was left and catch the bus home, they were all sat there, nodding in agreement with our decision.

"That was the tale of our camping trip. We're sorry about the tent George, it was really good of you to lend it to us." Having again thanked George, I quickly sat down.

I think our teacher had intended for the class to have a discussion about our camping trip and what it had entailed, but after I'd given my little talk and sat down, he had to change his plan. All he could do was to say how glad he was that none of us had got burnt and to stress to everyone about the dangers of fire.

As we were heading for the door, to go out for playtime, the lads all came up to me, quietly laughing and saying that my story was that realistic that they'd had to keep reminding themselves that it hadn't really happened.

When we got outside we were instantly surrounded by girls, asking us about the fire and telling us how brave we were. Naturally, as we each told them our tales, our stories got more and more exaggerated, so that by the time the bell went the flames had become thirty foot high, the heat of the fire was hotter than the sun and we'd each risked life and limb trying to put the tent out!

We were heroes!

Not only that, but some of the girls had made a point of telling George how kind he was to have lent us the tent and were offering him sympathy about it being destroyed. He was so pleased about the attention that he was receiving that he decided that he wasn't going to bash Peter after all.

Not a bad ending for a trip that had been a disaster and could have resulted in us being a laughing stock at school.

31
THE NEW DAM

When I was a young lad most of our fun involved laiking outside. When I was with the other lads, this generally involved activities like climbing trees, falling out of trees, (which was always a laugh for everyone except whoever had fallen that time), and creating havoc on our home made bogie. When I was on my own, I spent as much time as possible roaming the moor with my two trusted companions, my gun and my dog.

Today may have seemed like many other Saturdays, a hot, sunny day, with no school to worry about, but today was going to be very different.

I hadn't long been up, when Clive and Norman started banging impatiently on the kitchen door. Given the early hour and the urgency of the knocking, I hurried to open the door in case something was wrong.

"Come on Joe, let's go and have a look at the new dam." Clive said by way of greeting me.

"The new dam?" I replied.

"Aye, the one o'er the moor" Norman helpfully informed me.

"I know where it is!" I shouted, "but it's miles away, Norman, it would take us all day to get there."

The dam had been built over the last few years and Norman's dad had seen it and said that it was really big. It didn't take the lads long to get me on board and, with Meg trotting along beside us, we called to collect Maurice and then, with Norman telling us that he knew how to get there, 'cos his father had told him, we set off without further delay.

We walked for hours and still couldn't even see the dam. After the first hour, or so, we were all privately beginning to think that Norman had got us lost, but we said nowt. It was hard work walking over the moor in amongst the heather, especially with the sun belting down on you and, by now, we were all hot and sweaty. We trudged on for a while, but soon we were all voicing our discomfort and our concerns that Norman had got us lost.

Norman was having none of it. He insisted that he knew the way and, what's more, that we weren't far away and would be there before long.

An hour later, not only had we not reached the dam, we still couldn't even see it. Exhausted, we sat ourselves down amongst the heather, sure that we couldn't go any further. We hadn't thought to bring any food with us, but where we had sat was next to a stream on the moor, so we used our hands to scoop up water to drink. We were too tired to even waste any breath accusing Norman of getting us lost, so we just sat there.

We had plonked ourselves down just below a small hill and, after we'd been sitting there for a short while, Norman said he would look over the hill and see if he could see the dam. I think he was feeling guilty about getting us lost on the moor. None of us volunteered to go with him, we were all still too knackered, so we watched as he set off up the hill.

He'd only been gone for a few minutes, when we all heard him shouting. We looked up to see Norman, stood on the brow of the hill, waving his arms in the air.

"I've found it! Thou art ne'er seen 'owt like it, it's as big as a sea!" He shouted down to us.

Suddenly full of energy again, we all jumped up and ran up the hill to join Norman.

Now, I'd heard about the sea, but I'd never been to the seaside, but when I looked down at the dam I thought that that is what the sea must look like. It was so big it seemed to stretch for ever.

We all just stood and stared, mouths wide open. None of us had ever seen anything like it before. The water looked so blue and inviting, it was awesome.

"I told you me father said it was big," Norman said with authority, his position as leader for the day no longer under threat.

We walked down the hill towards the dam, climbing over the wall which surrounded it, whose purpose was to keep people and, more particularly, gangs of lads, like us, out. The boys gave me a hand to get Meg over the wall and, as soon as she was over, Meg raced down to the edge of the dam, launched herself into the water, and then started swimming.

As we all stood watching her and laughing, Meg swam over, climbed out and shook herself violently, soaking all of us.

"By, she enjoyed that swim." Clive said and we all agreed.

"Why don't we all go for a swim?" Maurice asked.

"We don't have any swimming trunks," I said.

"What difference will that make to you Joe? We've seen your bum and willy when you went swimming in Tinkle Beck with your Madge's white silk knickers on!"

We all laughed, but we were a few years older now and all felt a bit awkward about stripping off in front of each other, so for a few seconds we all just stood there.

"Nobody can see us, there's nobody for miles around and that water looks really nice."

Clive broke the silence and then, without further hesitation, started pulling off his clothes.

The rest of us didn't need any further persuasion and, in seconds, clothes were flying in all directions, as we raced to see who could be first into the water.

Free of our clothes, we ran down to the edge of the dam and jumped straight in. The water was freezing and the shock that we felt as we each went under the surface took our breath away. It's only now, looking back, that I realise how dangerous our little swim was. Whilst we could all swim, we were all used to being in places where we could stand up in the water, but here, the sides of the dam gave way to deep water. Swimming by a dam is never a good idea anyway, never mind for a group of lads who weren't particularly strong swimmers and who were risking hypothermia to boot.

At the time though none of that entered our heads and we swam, dived and splashed around excitedly. After a good ten minutes we scrambled out of the water, all looking clean, if a little blue. I was horrified and embarrassed to see that the cold water had made me willy all but disappear, but relaxed when I saw that the same thing had happened to all the others and that they were each looking around with the same expression on their faces.

We lay out on the bank of the dam, letting the sun warm our frozen bodies, whilst we had a bit of lads talk. We chatted about a few things, but mainly about the girls at school, who had pig tails and wore gym slips. We told tales about sitting behind the girls in the classroom and pulling their pig tails. The innocence of youth.

Once our bodies were warm and dry, someone asked if we were going in again, or getting dressed. We all remembered just how cold the water had been, so, as one, said that we weren't going back in. As we all started to put on our clothes, Norman, a serious look on his face, looked around us all.

"You know it's Keighley's drinking water, so I hope you lot didn't piss in it!"

"No," we all said, but each of us was looking down, sheepishly.

Realising that every one of us had peed in the water, we all started laughing.

We'd all been having such a good time and laughing so much, that none of us had noticed the black clouds that had filled the sky. The next instant we heard an enormous clap of thunder, followed immediately by a fork of lightning, and then the rain came down in buckets.

The only place to shelter was in the culvert, which was an arch brickwork tunnel that was used for letting overflowing water out of the dam. We ran to it as quickly as we could.

"Let's hope they don't let the dam off, or we will all be drowned." Clive helpfully informed us.

"Don't be daft, I 'aven't seen anybody working at the dam." Norman said, but he didn't sound very certain.

It was a bit scary standing in the culvert watching the thunder and lightning and marvelling at just how fast the rain was coming down. As time passed, we were all beginning to think that we might have to stay there all night, a thought that did nothing to reduce our fears.

Just as quickly as it had started though, the rain suddenly stopped.

As we all started the long walk back across the moor, our bravery restored, we agreed that it had been the biggest storm we had ever seen.

It was already late afternoon as we were setting off and, not having had anything to eat all day, we were all feeling really hungry and tired. We hadn't walked far when hunger took control, so we sat down in the heather and started picking bilberries. It wasn't long though until we got fed up with that, it's a slow job and it takes a lot of bilberries to fill your belly.

So, still hungry, we got back to our feet to continue the long walk home. Not only were we still hungry, but now we had wet backsides too, the result of sitting down in the heather.

No matter how tired, wet and hungry we were, as we walked back across the moor, we all agreed that today had been a good day and was just like what it must be like to be at the seaside. We all knew that we'd be in big trouble if people found out that we'd gone swimming in the dam, so we agreed not to tell anyone. After all, as we agreed, if none of us said anything there was no way that anyone could ever find out.

Our great plan to keep our secret and avoid punishment only had one small flaw, the fact that we all looked a lot cleaner coming back from the dam than we had looked setting off to go to it. Even Meg looked and smelled cleaner!

32
DEATH VISITS PONDHILL AGAIN

Most mornings at Pondhill started the same way. I would jump out of bed, have a pee in the jerry, and then me and Meg would run downstairs. I'd let Meg out for a pee and, while she was out, I'd wash my hands and face with cold water and clean my teeth at the stone sink in the kitchen.

The kitchen was the only room in the house with a fire and, no matter what time of year it was, the nights were usually cold and the bedrooms, which didn't really warm up much during the day because the thick stone walls kept the heat of the sun out, were freezing. That's why I did, literally jump out of bed and run downstairs. Sometimes, in winter, we'd put peat on the fire last thing at night and dampen it down with water, to stop it burning too quickly. That way, if we were lucky, the peat would still be burning in the morning and the kitchen would be warm.

If the peat was still burning, after I'd had my wash, I'd put some dry peat on the fire, to get it blazing, then fill the big cast iron kettle with water from the buckets I'd filled at the well the night before and put it on the range where, provided the fire in the range was blazing, it wouldn't take long to come to the boil.

In some ways, those winter mornings were the best, because I could get dressed in the warm, in front of the fire. For all it was so cold overnight, we couldn't keep the fire going in summer, because we had to keep the peat for winter fuel, so the kitchen was generally cold when we first came downstairs, albeit still warmer than the rest of the house.

With the fire blazing, the water boiling and me dressed, I would then get my breakfast. Usually this was a glass of milk and a piece of bread with jam on. Typically, while I was getting my breakfast, Meg would return, ready for her own breakfast.

That was what happened most mornings at Pondhill, but not that day, a day that I will never forget.

We'd got up and, as usual, I'd let Meg out, washed and dressed, got the fire blazing and put the kettle on, before getting my breakfast. Madge was putting her coat on to go to work, as I ate my bread and jam.

"Meg's not come back for her breakfast yet." I told her.

"Don't worry, I'm sure she'll be back in a minute, just you make sure that you get ready for school on time." Madge told me and, with a wave, she set off on her way to work.

Despite what Madge had said, I was worried. Meg always came back in after a few minutes. It wasn't like her not to be back, looking for her breakfast.

I went outside and called her.

I looked around the farm and down the fields, but I couldn't see her.

I shouted her name and whistled for her, but still she didn't come.

There was no way that I was going to school until I'd found her.

I spent all morning looking for her. I called at Ken's and, whilst telling me that he hadn't seen her, he did give me some advice.

"Find her quick, Joe, it's lambing time." The concern was written all over his face.

"She wouldn't touch a lamb." I had no hesitation in telling him.

Feeling sick, thinking she may be hurt somewhere, I walked back to the farm and sat on the doorstep, my head in my hands. I didn't know what else I could do.

I don't know how long I sat there, maybe only a few minutes, but all of a sudden something was licking my face.

"Meg, oh where have you been girl?" I cried, as I put my arms around her.

Hugging her to me, I became aware of something wet and sticky on my hand. Blood.

Straight away I started checking Meg, to see where her injury was. There wasn't one.

My mind instinctively told me what had happened and my joy at having her back with me turned to sheer terror.

"Oh Meg, what have you done."

Even as I muttered to her I was getting to my feet and pulling her over to the well.

I got a bucket of water and washed the blood from Meg's coat.

With legs like jelly and with my heart pounding so hard it threatened to rip through my chest, we ran into the house.

As I sat there, praying that nobody had seen her, Meg sat in front of the fire, drying herself. Each time I looked at her she started wagging her tail, totally unaware of the danger she'd put herself in. All afternoon we sat there, too scared to risk venturing out.

Just when I was beginning to think that nobody had seen her. Just when my heartbeat was starting to return to something like normal. Just when my legs had stopped trembling, Meg started to growl quietly.

Looking out of the window, I saw what I had dreaded seeing since I'd found the blood on Meg's coat.

Walking down the lane, towards the farm, came Mr Jackson, with his gun under his arm.

We both waited for the knock on the door and, when it came neither of us moved, or made a sound.

Hoping that he would just go away, we continued to ignore the knocking on the door, as, holding Meg close to me, I crawled under the table to hide.

He didn't go away.

"Come on now Joe, I know you're in there!" he shouted.

I'll never know how my legs managed to carry me across the floor to answer the door, but somehow they did.

I opened the door and heard a voice similar to mine.

"What do you want, Mr Jackson?"

"You know what I have come for, Joe. Your dog was seen worrying lambs this morning."

"No, Mr Jackson, Meg's been with me all morning." I didn't want to lie, but I had to save Meg.

"Now young Joe, you know that's not true. Two dogs were seen this morning worrying Mr Greenwood's lambs and Mr Greenwood knew both dogs. I've already put the other one down."

"No, you can't!" I yelled.

"Joe, Mr Greenwood says he won't charge you for the lambs, but your dog has to be put down."

"No, I won't let you do it, I love her and she's my best friend!" I shouted at him.

Ignoring my pleading, Mr Jackson started to step forward into the kitchen, to get Meg.

Desperate, I grabbed the poker and, holding it aloft, screamed "If you come near Meg, I'll kill you!" I think he was surprised and shocked at my outburst.

Mr Jackson stopped and took a step back. No kid had ever spoken to him like that before, certainly not Maurice.

He looked at me for a few seconds. When he spoke again his voice was kind, but firm.

"Now look, Joe, I know you are upset, but you live in the countryside and you know the law - if it's worried once, it'll do it again."

There was no reasoning with me. I was screaming, shouting and yelling at him. Waving the poker in the air around me, I told him not to come near Meg, my words coming out amongst my sobs and cries.

Mr Jackson just looked at me. I don't think he knew what to do, but in the end he told me that he would give me ten minutes to calm down, then I had to bring Meg out or he would have to fetch the police.

With that, he turned, left the farmhouse and walked a few steps away before waiting.

I sat with my arms round Meg, telling her how much I loved her and that she was my best friend. I was crying and sobbing uncontrollably, the tears running down my cheeks. Meg looked sadly up at me and started to lick the tears from my cheeks.

I knew that I had no choice but to take her outside. If he called the police, Meg would still be made to meet her fate and it would cause a whole load more trouble for us besides, but it was the hardest thing I have ever had to do.

I was blinded by the tears in my eyes, as I stood on legs of jelly and pulled Meg up onto her feet. I don't know how we made it to the door but, as I opened it and stepped outside, my legs gave way.

I was on my knees, holding Meg on her lead when, without warning, I heard the bang of the gun being fired and, in that instant, there was blood everywhere.

"Next time tha' gets a dog, tha'd better look after it."

Mr Jackson looked down at me and said, before he turned and walked away.

I was still cradling Meg when Madge arrived home.

"What are you doing sitting on the cold stone flags, Joe, you'll catch your death of cold." Madge said as she walked towards us, then she saw Meg.

"Oh, Joe, what's happened?"

Madge held me tight as I fell into her arms. My whole body racked with sobs, as I told Madge what had happened to Meg.

Madge was crying too as I asked her, in between sobs, why everything that I had ever loved has been taken away from me, Mam, Dad and now even Meg.

Madge had no answer, other than to hold me close to her as we both continued to cry.

Eventually, my sobs died down enough for me to speak again.

"Help me to bury her, Madge. I want to put her behind the pig hole, so she can see the moor and be in the sun."

Both of us in tears, we started to dig Meg's grave. It was hard digging for two youngsters, but, after about two hours, the grave was ready.

We wrapped Meg in a sack and put her in the grave, and then covered her over with soil. I picked some daisies and buttercups and put them on the grave.

Madge gave me another hug, then left me to be alone with Meg.

I sat by the grave until long after it became dark, not wanting to leave my best friend.

Going to bed that night without Meg, was awful.

I could still smell her on the bedclothes. I lay there, heartbroken, thinking over and over that if only I had not let her out that morning she would still be here with me.

I don't know how I got through the next few days without Meg. The pain that I felt was just like it had been when I lost my Mam.

When I went back to school a week later, everyone knew that Meg had been shot and the class teacher and all the other kids, not just my mates, were very sympathetic and went out of their way to try to make me feel better.

As kind as they were and as much as they helped to take my mind off things during the day, they couldn't do anything to take away the pain that started in my belly each day as I was going home from school and Meg was not there to run out and meet me.

"Pondhill Farm, taken some time after it had been renovated in the 1960's"

"Kids digging peat for winter fuel"

"Bringing the peat home from the moors"

"Tinkler Beck, as it passes Pondhill
Farm"

"A typical cooking range, similar to what we had at
Pondhill. This photo is of the range in the Old Hall Inn,
at Threshfield (well worth a visit – Joyce and I eat there
every time we go back to Yorkshire)"

"The severe winter of 1947"

"Curly Blackburn's house, which we covered with peat sods"

"Me and Clive, dressed up for the Cowling gala fancy dress competition"

"Here I am sitting on 'Tommy', who I took to school"

"Madge, after we'd lost Mam and Dad and were at Pondhill on our own"

"Another view of the moors, where I hunted for my food and where Clive and I went joyriding. Cuckoo Rock can be seen in the top right hand third of the photo"

"Me with Meg, my best friend and constant companion"

33
A REALLY CRAP JOB

The days passed and turned into weeks, but the pain of losing Meg stayed with me. Going to bed at night without her, and then waking up in the mornings and Meg not being there were the worst times. I felt like something had died inside of me.

However much Madge, Clive and Norman tried to comfort me, it didn't work. My friendship with Maurice was also 'on hold' throughout that time. Meg's shooting had been nothing to do with Maurice, but, as it was his father who had shot her, part of me blamed him anyway. Maurice knew this, and also felt embarrassed because of what his father had done and the fact that he didn't know what he should say to me, so he kept his distance.

As the saying goes, life goes on, and I still had to go out onto the moors to shoot for food, but it just wasn't the same anymore. Whereas I used to talk to Meg all the time we were hunting for our dinner, now I would sit in the heather sobbing my heart out, unable to stop thinking about Meg and feeling so lost and empty without her. I knew that the constant crying wasn't helping me and that I had to pull myself together, but knowing it and doing it were different things. I needed something to occupy me, so that I didn't have time just to sit and think about Meg, and all of a sudden, one day, something did happen – I got a job!

Matthew Dawson, a local farmer in the village, had heard about Meg and knew how upset I was. He told me that if I helped him after school each day and on Saturday mornings, he would give me sixpence a week. I jumped at the chance to have some money in my pocket. Before I'd even started I was already planning what I would spend it on.

Now back in the forties and fifties, farming was hard work for little return, so most farmers took on extra jobs to earn a bit more money for their family. Like most farmers, Matthew was a big strong chap and, again like most people in those days, he was always ready to help others. I knew what Matthew's spare time job was when he asked me to help him, but I still said yes.

He worked for the local council as a collector of human waste from the dry outside toilets, or, as we kids used to call him, he was the shit collector!

He only collected the waste from around the village, as on the farms they put it on the land as fertiliser. So, on my first Saturday morning, we set off in his horse and cart down to the village. The cart was a tipper, with large sides and a door at the back which would open.

Compared to what people had on the farms, toilets in the houses in the village were really posh. They were still outside, but they each had a bucket under the closet seat to contain the waste. Our job was to collect the bucket, empty it into the cart, and then put it back.

The first rule that Matthew told me was to make sure that I called out, to let anyone who happened to be on the closet know that we were going to empty the bucket.

"You don't want to catch anyone having a shit, young Joe."

He told me this very 'matter of factly' and with a serious face, but I couldn't stop myself from grinning at the thought!

Now, if only one person lived in a house, the bucket wouldn't have much in it, but if it was a big family, the bucket would be overflowing. We also knew who was suffering from stomach upsets at any given time! What made our task even worse was the fact that we didn't have gloves, overalls, or face masks!

When the cart was full, we would climb up front and set off to empty it in what we called the delph holes. The delph holes were just big rocky holes in the sloping sides of the steep fields that were just outside the village. Health and Safety was barely considered in those days, and nobody seemed to think there was anything wrong with using the delph holes for dumping all that we'd collected, even though when it rained the shit would flow out of the hole and down the hillside into Ickornshaw Beck and continue into the rivers around the village!

Anyway, my job on the way to the delph holes was to keep an eye on the back door of the cart, to make sure it didn't start swinging open. Normally there wasn't a problem, but one day the door swung open just as Matthew was turning the cart to leave the road. There was shit everywhere and it took me all day to clean the stinking mess up, with Matthew shouting at me that I should have been watching the door so that I could have warned him to stop.

Normally though, we'd arrive at the delph hole with the cart door still intact. We'd then dismount and lead the horse backwards, until the cart was angled over the edge of the hole. Then Matthew would open the door and the contents of the cart would slop out into the hole. The stench when this was happening was horrendous, but it didn't bother me too much and so, as soon as we'd dumped our load, we'd get back on the cart, return to the village and start again at the next street.

Just about everyone knew Matthew and often people would call out a cheery hello, or make reference to him having his little helper with him. Sometimes we were even offered a drink – Matt, as he preferred to be called would always ask for a cup of tea, whereas I always asked for a glass of milk. I found myself copying Matt's habit of taking a long drink, then wiping his mouth with the back of his hand.

It never crossed our minds to wash our hands before having our drinks!

Matt told me I was a good worker and I helped him for a few weeks. I did manage to save a few pence out of my sixpence a week, but my craving for cigarettes meant that most of the money was spent very quickly. It would be years later before I decided that smoking was a complete waste of my hard earned money, as well as being bad for your health.

As much as I didn't mind the work that we had to do and as much as I liked getting my sixpence a week, my work with Matt came to a sudden stop.

This particular day, it had been pouring all day and was still raining hard as we headed out of the village with another load of crap on the cart. As we started up the hill, all the shit in the back of the cart was getting very wet and sloppy and was swirling about the cart more and more with every turn of the wheels, such that it was soon in danger of slopping over the sides.

Matt told me to get the shovel and try to keep it all in the cart. Well, you can imagine what a job that was and it's fair to say that by the time we'd got over the fields there was as much shit on me as we tipped into the delph hole!

It was a Saturday and when I got back to Pondhill Madge was home. She swore that she could smell me long before I'd come into sight and she made me strip off at the door.

Boy was she not happy, and she let me know by continuously shouting at me, telling me how daft I was and how much I stank, as she got the tin bath out and boiled up water to fill it.

She was still shouting at me as I got in the bath, telling me to make sure I put my clothes in the water to soak after I'd got out.

That Saturday night, as I sat wrapped in a blanket waiting for my clothes to dry, Madge banned me from helping Matt again. She was that mad at me that it never even entered my mind to argue with her.

So that was the end of that job. I missed going with Matt and, looking back, there's no doubt that it had helped me to get over Meg. I have never forgotten her, but when I talked to Matt about her, he'd said that I had to make sure that I thought about all the good times we had spent together, so that I filled my head with happy memories, not sad ones.

He was right.

34
KEN AND EDNA – MY PRETEND FAMILY

Having lost Mam, Dad and then also Meg, I often felt very lonely. This was particularly the case during winter when, as I came home from school, the house would look very cold, dark and forbidding. How I longed for the days when Mam had been there to make sure there was a welcoming light in the window and that a fire was lit in the grate.

But Mam wasn't there anymore. I would make my lonely approach and quickly fix a light to stave off the oppressive darkness. More often than not, I would have to go out searching for firewood, before I could light a fire to provide some warmth and a little more light. With the fire set, I would take the water bucket to fill it from the well, and then put some water on to heat up.

All too often, the cupboards were bare. Not much more than a kid herself, Madge often prioritised her blossoming social life ahead of doing any shopping. On such winter's nights, I would have to venture out with only my gun for company, to try and find something that I could shoot to eat. It being winter made this task even harder than usual, because as well as it being cold and dark, most animals had gone to ground for the winter, so pickings were hard to come by.

As much as I loved Madge, on such winter's evenings I used to grumble about her to myself as, cold, scared and hungry, I hunted my dinner.

How I envied all the other kids, who still had mams and dads.

Throughout my adult years, when talking with people about my childhood, several of them have remarked that it's a wonder that I didn't stray off the straight and narrow. I can understand why people might have thought that it would have been easy for a lad in my situation to stray down a slippery path into petty crime and whatever that led to. What those people didn't take into account was the one thing that meant that such a career choice was never going to be an option for me – my Mam.

Mam had always instilled in me the importance of being honest, hard-working and respectful to others. Her passing when I was still so young, coupled with losing Dad first to illness and then through his death, could have meant that these lessons were forgotten, except for one simple fact, which is that Mam may not have been there physically, but she never left me.

In everything I did, I would think about what Mam would have said and thought about it. I would hear her confirming to me what I already knew, which was whether what I was doing was right or wrong. I can't remember a time while I was growing up that I ever doubted that the voice I heard inside my head was Mam keeping an eye on me. If I ever had doubted it though, the following event would soon have put me right.

One day, after school, instead of going straight home to the cold and dark house that awaited me, I went over to Ethel's, to see Val. It was a long walk, but, since Meg had died, I didn't have anything better to do. We played football for a while, until Val had to go home, at which point I started the long walk home.

As usual, I was cold and hungry and, feeling sorry for myself, was bemoaning the fact that I never had money to buy the food that Madge all too often forgot that we needed. As I walked along I saw that the lamp lighter was starting to light the old gas lamps that used to light the streets. I knew that the lamp heads would fetch good money and, without thinking things through as I normally would, I decided that if I took one I'd be able to feed well for days.

I went round the next corner and, seeing that the street was empty, stopped and stared at one of the gas lamps, thinking only of how good it would feel to have a full belly for a few days.

"Oy, what are you up to?"

The shout from the lamp lighter made me jump like the rabbits used to when they turned to see Meg charging towards them.

For all that I had not done anything wrong at that time, I started to run and, once I'd started, I just kept going. I didn't look behind to see if I was being chased or not, I just ran. Finally, my legs had no more strength and my lungs were bursting through my chest so, knowing I couldn't run another step, I leapt over the wall that was then beside me.

I landed on grass and, gasping for air, rolled over a few times to take me away from the wall and into the shadows so that, if I was being followed it would be harder to see me.

Crouched there, trying to slow my breathing, which I was sure could be heard a mile away, I looked around and realised that I'd jumped into the cemetery. I looked at the stone nearest to me, already knowing what it was going to say.

It was my Mam's grave.

I was at once both ashamed that I'd even allowed myself the thought of taking one of the gas lamps and angry at myself because if I'd done such a thing it would have upset my Mam.

As I said before, if ever I'd doubted that my Mam was still watching over me and influencing me, that night would cast away those doubts for ever.

*

Sometimes though things would all get on top of me and I'd feel particularly down and lonely. When I felt like this I would go across to see Ken and Edna and pretend that they were my family. They always managed to cheer me up and, looking back, they were like family to me and without them things may well have been very different for Madge and me.

One Saturday, Ken asked me if I would like to go off for the day with him to Barnoldswick, where he was going to buy a land motor. Up until then, Ken had done all his hay making by hand. He would load his sledge with hay, then tie a rope around the sledge and pull it by hand across the fields back to the barn. He'd continue this process all day long, until the field was cleared of hay. Sometimes I'd help him, loading the hay onto the sledge, and I would wince at the sight of Ken's back by the end of the day. He would be streaked with blood, with deep, open sores across his back and shoulders from where the rope had dug into him as he'd pulled the heavily loaded sledge. I can't help but wonder about what Ken would make of all the modern farming machinery available these days.

Anyway, back to that Saturday morning, and off we went, walking down the lane to take the bus to Colne, where we had to change buses to catch a bus for Barnoldswick.

When we got off in Colne, we had about half an hour to wait for our next bus and, as it was a very hot day, we just sat down on the pavement. Ken remarked about how hot it was and took off his flat cap, putting it down on the ground beside him.

Within a few minutes of us sitting down, people started throwing money into his cap. We both gasped, looked at the cap, and then looked at each other.

"People think we're beggars!"

As soon as we said it, we both started laughing. Mind you, thinking back, I think we probably both looked like beggars, with me in my cast-off suit and Ken not much better.

We were still laughing when Ken said that we should buy ice-creams with the money we'd been given. He did though make me promise not to tell Edna that we'd been mistaken for beggars. When the bus for Barnoldswick arrived, we went and sat upstairs, eating our ice-creams and still laughing about being taken for beggars.

We were still chuckling when we arrived at the farm where the land motor was for sale. It was just an old car with the back cut off and boards laid out in the back, so you could put hay, or anything else in the back, to save you from carrying and pulling it yourself. The gears were gate changed and there were no brakes, which was a bit of a worry, as Ken was going to drive it home!

After about twenty minute of bartering, a deal was done and Ken was now the proud owner of the motor. He looked really pleased with himself as he winked at me and said "Wuth dun alreet yonder."

Looking back, the motor was a monstrosity, but for Ken it was a godsend, as it would save him a lot of hard work.

How to describe the journey home?

Driving through the town was hazardous, an adventure, perilous, exciting and frightening, all at the same time. Having no brakes, Ken had to judge when to ease off the accelerator, such that we'd stop in time for traffic lights, or road junctions, and at the same time we had to hope that no police would be on duty at any of the junctions.

Having made it through the town and out onto the open road, Ken decided to 'open her up and see what she'll do!'

"Let's see how fast she can go, Joe!" Ken shouted, as he opened her up as far as she'd go.

I think we got her up to about 30 mph.

As slow as that now seems, at the time, to me, we were flying and as our excitement mounted so did my fear – the thought that there were no brakes never leaving my mind. Ken got that excited that he started to sing, although I now wonder whether that was his way of hiding his own fear.

Somehow, more by luck than judgement, we made it home safe and in one piece. As Edna came out to see the motor, Ken again reminded me not to mention having been mistaken for beggars.

At first, Edna was really pleased and excited about the motor. That was until she wanted to go for a drive and Ken told her that there weren't any brakes, so she'd have to wait until he repaired them.

"You mean that you drove yourself and Joe all the way back in that thing with no brakes?"

Edna's face darkened as she rounded on Ken and I took that as my cue to beat a hasty retreat, so shouting my goodbyes and my thanks back over my shoulder, I ran back to Pondhill.

35
THE BIRDS & THE BEES
AND A NEW ARRIVAL AT PONDHILL

When I was fourteen and in my last year at school, I remember that I couldn't wait to finally leave school forever.

I would sit and tell myself, "only nine more months to go, then I can get a job and have money to buy new clothes instead of always wearing someone else's cast-offs".

The more I was growing up, the more aware I was of my clothes and how they must make me look to other people. Clive and I had started to take an interest in girls, and although we were never short of lasses' company, I never really thought I had a chance with any of them, even though Clive always complained that the good looking ones were always interested in me and not him. The way I looked at it, I would never stand a chance with them as long as I looked like I'd been dressed from the rag bag.

Given what had happened to our Mam and Dad, and the fact that we'd lived alone since losing them, Madge and me had always been close and looked after each other. I knew that Madge had boyfriends and didn't really mind, even though I always hoped that she would get off with Norman.

Then, one day, Madge told me that she was bringing a boyfriend home.

"Yeah, okay", I said with little interest in what she was saying.

My interest was certainly there a moment later, when she went on to say that he would be living here!

"You can't let him live here, Madge! What would Mam say? Who is he and how long have you known him? You're only seventeen!"

Despite my outburst, Madge had made up her mind. She said that he was very good looking and that she was in love with him and he loved her. He was in the army, but would be coming out in about two weeks' time, at which time he would be moving in.

Over the next two weeks I tried everything I could think of to talk her out of letting him live at the farm. No matter what I said, or how many times I said it, Madge remained adamant that he would be moving in.

Realising that I was not going to change her mind, I cheered myself up by convincing myself that when he arrived and saw that we had no running water, gas or electric and that we had an outside closet, he would not want to stay.

My hope turned out to be totally misplaced. One Saturday morning I got up to find Madge was already downstairs, cleaning the kitchen, something she hadn't done for a long time.

"What are you up early, doing that for?" I asked her.

"I want it to be nice for when Joe arrives, he's coming today", Madge happily replied.

"Did tha' just say that he's called Joe?" I couldn't believe what I'd heard.

"Aye, he's called Joe Crumack and he'll be here soon".

Even though I'm sure that I didn't sound pleased to hear of the imminent arrival of the boyfriend, or that he shared my name, Madge was too happy to pick up on it and just carried on cleaning with a big grin on her face.

As I watched her happily going about her work, I sat fuming about the intruder who would soon arrive. Not only was he about to share our lives and home, but on top of that he went by my name. I decided there and then that I would never call him Joe. If I was forced to speak to him, or refer to him, then Crumack was all that I'd call him!

A short time later he arrived and I got the shock of my life when he walked through the kitchen door. Whatever else I'd been thinking, I'd expected Crumack to be a young man. This man was old - he must have been at least thirty! What was Madge thinking of.

Madge was fussing all over him straight away. He was tall, with dark hair and he was good looking, but in a sleazy sort of way. I could see that he had a good opinion of himself, the way he came into the kitchen and made himself at home straight away.

"Come on love, make me a pot of tea", he said to Madge, who immediately set about doing what he'd asked. Next, he turned to me.

"Now Joe, I'm going to look after you, so you won't have anything to worry about again".

Him, Crumack, look after me! Was he joking?

The minute that he walked into the kitchen, I took an instant dislike to the man and knew that Madge was making a terrible mistake. Sadly, as the years passed, I was proved to be right.

With the arrival of Crumack at Pondhill, I spent more time with Ken and Edna, or, after school, I would call in at Ada and Johnny's. Ada wasn't pleased about Crumack moving into Pondhill and hoped that Madge would come to her senses and kick him out.

Clive, Maurice and Norman thought that he was full of bullshit and I totally agreed with them.

Despite all this, there was nothing that me, or anyone else could do. I just hoped, like Ada, that Madge would get fed up with him and send him packing.

"Maybe, if he has a winter at Pondhill, he may decide to leave" I thought, but, as winter was still six months away, even this thought didn't cheer me up.

Clive's father was quite small in build, which Clive took after, and was quite quiet and shy – which Clive definitely did not take after!

Anyway, Clive's dad had noticed that we had started taking an interest in the girls, and, with me not having a father, he decided that he should give us both a talk about the birds and the bees.

Clive's home, called The Mount, was a nice, little, homely cottage, but it was out of the village a good way up Cowling Hill. One Saturday morning, after peddling up Cowling hill on my tandem, I arrived at The Mount, to see Clive waiting for me and laughing his head off.

"What's up?" I said.

"It's me father, he's going to tell us about the birds and the bees!"

Clive spluttered through his laughter. Now it was my turn to burst out laughing.

After we'd just about got ourselves back under control, and struggling to put serious expressions on our faces, we walked into the kitchen, where Clive's dad was waiting for us. I'll never forget how worried and on edge Clive's old man looked, the poor man had got himself into a right state.

"Right lads," he started as we sat down, "I think it's time that we had a talk. Joe, you not having parents, I've put it on myself to include you in this."

"What are we having a talk about, Mr Paley?" I innocently asked, noticing Clive's body shaking as he struggled to keep in his laughter.

"I'm going to give you some advice about girls, you have to be very careful when you take a girl out," Clive's dad stammered.

"What do you mean 'we have to be careful', Mr Paley?" I said, and this time I joined Clive in desperately trying not to let the laughter burst out.

Clive's dad stood up, moved from foot to foot, and coughed and cleared his throat, before continuing.

"Well, you know," he finally said.

"No, we don't know. What do you mean father?" Clive said, somehow just managing to keep a straight face.

"Well, you don't want to get them into trouble, do you?"

Mr Paley was wearing the face of a man who wished he'd never started the conversation.

"Oh no, don't worry, we won't get them into trouble."

A look of hope entered Mr Paley's eyes as he heard this and thought that he might yet get out of this conversation without having to say more. That look of hope vanished as quickly as it had appeared, as we both continued to say, "we won't get them into trouble, because we don't let them smoke."

"I'm not talking about smoking!" Whilst he had raised his voice, it was more in desperation and frustration than anger.

"Well if you're not talking about smoking, how else can we get a lass into trouble?" I asked him, enjoying watching the poor man struggle.

Looking back, we made him feel so uncomfortable and embarrassed that it's to his eternal credit that he kept going and managed to explain anything to us. Whether or not he realised that we were mucking him about, I don't know, but I do know that he had the last laugh.

After a long discussion about what lads and lasses do, during which me and Clive played dumb to everything, so that the poor man was forced to go into details that I swear made him blush, he told us about what would happen if we went with a 'mucky woman'.

The way he described the disease that we could get 'down below' frightened us that much that for a long time afterwards we hardly dared even take our willies out to pee!

The trouble was, he didn't explain what he meant by a mucky woman and, worse still, whilst he'd made sure that we knew that the disease was something awful, he didn't actually tell us what happened if you caught it – leaving our imaginations to run wild!

"Heck, Clive, if you got something like your father told us about, your willy could fall off!"

"Blinking heck, Joe, I didn't know that you could get a disease like that on your willy!"

Usually, as we rode the tandem down into the village we would encourage each other to race down the hill at full speed. That day, we rolled along quite slowly, both deep in thought and worried for the future of our willies.

When we cycled into the village, we bumped into Maurice and Norman.

"What's up with you two? You look a bit down in the mouth, have you lost a sixpence? Norman said.

"No," I said, "but do you know about the disease that you can get from mucky women, when your willy can fall off?"

"Eh?" Norman's mouth fell open, "who told you that?"

"Me father. It's true." Clive told him, in a voice that didn't leave it open to question.

Now I don't think Norman did know about the disease, but being older he wasn't going to admit to us that he didn't know about something that we had heard of.

"Well, I had heard summat about it," he said after a few seconds of thought.

For the next hour or so we talked about the disease and lasses.

"Maybe you should ask your father about the disease, Norman", I started to suggest, but Norman stopped me in my tracks before I could add anything else.

"If I asked me father that I would get a clout round ear hole!"

As desperate as we all were to find out more about the disease, we realised that no matter how long the three of us talked, we wouldn't know anything more. So, reluctantly, we made our way home.

As I was cycling home, I couldn't stop thinking about the disease. I couldn't risk my willy falling off – I had to find out more! All of a sudden, I thought about Ken, he was bound to know about it. There was no time to waste, as soon as I got home I'd go round and ask him.

When I got there, Ken was working in the farm yard. As desperate as I was to learn more about the disease, even I struggled to just blurt the question straight out, so I slowly made my way over to him and started making small talk.

"What are you doing, Ken?"

"Just finding rubbish to burn on the range." Ken replied, without stopping.

"Oh, right", I couldn't think of what to say.

Now Ken knew me as well as anyone and could tell by my lack of chat and by the frown that I was wearing that something was bothering me.

"So, what are you up to?" he asked.

"Nothing really"

"Come on Joe, I know something's bothering you, so just spit it out."

Ken had stopped working and was looking me straight in the eye.

I was too embarrassed to look at him, so my eyes bored into his feet as I took a deep breath and told him what was bothering me.

"Clive's father was telling us about lads and lasses and how we shouldn't get them in trouble," I started. "Then he told us about the disease we can get on our willies if we go with a mucky woman and me and Clive are worried 'cos we've already kissed a couple of girls each already and we don't want our willies to fall off!"

Once I started telling him, the words just spilled out of me and I didn't pause for breath until they were all out.

Ken looked at me and, for a few seconds, said nothing. Then he burst out laughing and ruffled my hair with one of his huge hands.

"So all of you young lads have been worrying that if you kiss and cuddle a lass your willies will fall off."

He spluttered through his laughter. "You daft young buggers!"

As his laughter died down, Ken told me to sit down and he'd explain things to me.

"First off, Joe," he said, "You won't get any disease on your willy from having a kiss and cuddle!"

He went on to explain things in a way I'd understand – by using farm animals as an example.

"You know what happens when you bring a bull to the cow?"

"Of course I do," I said.

"Well, men and women do that too, but, if a man is always going with different woman, and a woman is going out with lots of different men and they're doing what the bull and cows do, that's when you can get the disease."

He also told me about what treatment you had to have if you got such a disease.

For all the treatment sounded really painful, I was so pleased to have heard what he'd told me.

"What a relief," I said, "Clive's father made us think if we had a pee in a public toilet we would get the disease and our willies could fall off!"

Ken was still laughing when I left him, but I couldn't hang about – I had to get to the lads and share the vital knowledge that I'd learnt.

36
I KISS SCHOOL GOODBYE

With autumn coming to an end and winter just round the corner, Crumack was still at the farm. If anything, my dislike of that man had grown even more intense. This was partly due to the fact that he acted as if the farm belonged to him, but, more so because he had started to boss Madge about. I regularly spoke to Madge about it, letting her know in no uncertain terms that I didn't like how he treated her, but, to my dismay, she always defended him, saying that him bossing her around was only a bit of fun and insisting that they loved each other.

I'd always thought that Madge had plenty of sense and so couldn't understand how she could be taken in by a man like Crumack.

Day by day, week by week, my dislike for him grew, as did my frustration that things showed no sign of changing any time soon. It wasn't long before my frustration was given the opportunity to show itself as anger.

All of the walking I did across the moors meant that I was relatively fit and I'd also grown quite tall since I'd hit my teens. On top of that, all of the work that I'd done over the last year helping farmers on their land hadn't just resulted in me having a few coins every now and then to keep myself in fags, but also in me developing a fair deal of muscle and strength to go with my fitness and height.

This one particular day, something had upset Crumack and he was in a foul mood. As I walked into the kitchen, he shouted at me to wipe my feet. Naturally, I ignored him and carried on walking across the room, but, as I walked past him, he grabbed hold of my arm.

Before he could say or do anything else I span round to face him and glared straight into his eyes. All my pent up anger suddenly surfaced.

"Get your hand off my arm!"

The guttural growl had come from my mouth, but even I didn't recognise the voice as belonging to me.

My eyes didn't leave his for a moment, as I felt his hand instantly release my arm. I don't know what would have happened if he'd resisted my challenge, but if my new found courage needed any encouragement, he gave it to me by backing off.

Still glaring at him, I told him in no uncertain terms exactly what I thought of him, before reminding him that Madge and me owned the farm.

"It's allus bin so, an' ivver will be, so don't forget you're only a lodger!"

I'd resisted the urge to hit him, but he would not forget that a fourteen year old lad had humiliated him in front of Madge.

Finally, I released him from my stare and turned to walk out of the kitchen. As I went, I looked across at Madge, who was standing open mouthed, not quite believing what had just happened.

"He's coddin you, Madge" was all that I said before I continued on out of the room.

I went and sat in our gang hut, wishing I had a cig to smoke, as I went back over what I'd done and wondered what would have happened if he hadn't backed off. I was still sat there a while later when Norman came in.

"What's up wi' thee, Joe?"

"Nowt to fret abaht," I said.

"Summat's up" Norman insisted and kept probing until I gave in and told him.

"Bugger me, Joe, he could have knocked bags of shit out of thee!"

"Well he didn't, did he? He backed off."

I could still feel the anger in my stomach as I spoke to Norman.

"He's bad news that Crumack, Joe, watch your back."

Norman's voice was full of genuine concern.

After a few seconds, during which I could feel the knot of anger in my stomach finally starting to unwind, I looked across at Norman.

"I wish Madge had fancied you, Norman, instead of that Crumack. It would have been alreet you living at Pondhill."

Norman just laughed and didn't say anything.

After my run in with Crumack we kept out of each other's way. After school I would go to Ada and John's and when I told Ada what had happened she was angry.

"If he lays a hand on you, I'll kill the bugger!" she hissed and, given the look on her face, I think she really meant it.

Madge was still awkward with me for telling Crumack that he was a lodger, but I didn't care. If she was so daft to be taken in with him, then that was her problem.

Any time during the weekends that the local farmers had no work for me, I would wander across the moors with my gun. Due to it being colder now, just about everything had gone to ground, but sometimes I would get a rabbit or a snipe. Grouse too was still in season, until the tenth of December, but even if grouse was out of season, if I was hungry I would shoot it.

I only had a few more weeks of having to go to school, as I would be fifteen on the nineteenth of December, at which time I could leave, so I started to think about getting a job. Everyone, lads and lasses, went into the mill when they left school, with the lucky ones getting a job weaving, which paid more money. After I'd told Ada that I was looking to get myself a job, she asked one of her neighbours, who just happened to be a manager at the mill, if he could sort something out for me.

Not only did he give me a job, he gave me a pair of overalls as well. I think he thought I would look a bit better in overalls than my own stuff which, as I've previously said, only loosely fitted the description of clothes. He also gave me a starting date – straight after Christmas.

With Christmas only a few weeks away, I had been trying to save some money from what I got from working with the farmers. I wanted to buy Madge some chocolates, now that rationing had finally ended after fourteen years.

I remember the day rationing, which had been in existence since I was a baby, ended. Clive, Maurice, Norman and me joined the long queue that had formed outside the sweet shop, waiting our turn and hoping that the shop hadn't sold out before we got served. When, at last, we got to the front of the queue, we just stood and stared open mouthed at all the sweets and chocolate on the shelves.

The shop was full of jars of different kinds of sweets and bars and boxes of different kinds of chocolate. We'd never seen anything like it in our lives.

Unable to resist, I bought a bar of chocolate and immediately tore the wrapper off, before greedily gobbling it down. I wasn't used to eating chocolate, so eating so much, so quickly, made me feel sick, but it tasted that good that it was worth it.

Knowing that I soon would be leaving there for good, I was even less interested in school than usual and had been regularly having days off throughout November and December, as my release date approached. However, there was one day I was determined not to miss – the day of the Christmas party. As was the tradition, all the lasses would bring mistletoe, giving all of the lads the perfect excuse to go around kissing them!

I was really looking forward to that, but I also had a bigger plan for the party.

"So what's the big plan, Joe?" Clive asked for the umpteenth time, as we sat chatting with Peter and Andrew.

"It's simple," I told them, "I'm going to kiss Miss Brown."

Now Miss Brown, our teacher, was young and fit and all the lads, including me, dreamed about her.

My friends were shocked and tried to talk me out of it, warning of being summoned to the headmaster and worse, but I'd made up my mind.

Come the Christmas party, I was armed with a piece of mistletoe and was ready to carry out my plan. I'd seen at the pictures how each of the big film stars get hold of the woman round her waist, bend her backwards and then kiss her, and that what I was going to do.

As I started walking around, to find her, the lads looked on in a mix of amazement and fear, waiting to see if I would dare to go through with my plan and if I'd get slapped, or worse, for my trouble.

I saw Miss Brown talking to some lasses, so went straight over to her. Without any hesitation, I held the mistletoe above her head, got hold of her round her waist, bent her backwards and gave her a long kiss. When finally our lips parted, I let her go and waited for the sound and pain that would be the features of my face slapping. I waited, then waited a little more, but it didn't come.

Instead of slapping me, Miss Brown sort of smiled and looked around with a surprised look on her face, which had gone a bit pink. The whole class had gone quiet, as they were all in shock at what they had just seen.

I looked at Miss Brown, smiled, and said "Merry Christmas."

"And the same to you, Joe," she said, as she smiled back at me.

I think she enjoyed the kiss, I know I did.

Walking back to the lads, I was grinning like a Cheshire cat.

"Bloody hell, Joe, we didn't think you would really kiss her!" the lads said, their eyes still wide open through shock at what they'd seen.

"Told you I would," I said to them, as suddenly I was surrounded by my class mates, all wanting to know how I'd dared to kiss Miss Brown and what it was like to kiss her. I felt like the cat who'd got the cream and remember thinking that it had been the best Christmas party, ever!

37
A Short Career at the Mill

It's funny how the simple things can sometimes be the best.

A hand bell ringing – to anyone else that's all that it was, but to me it was one of the sweetest things I'd ever heard. People may not have realised it, but that bell was saying that Joe Sawley's school days were over, for good.

When it started ringing on that wonderful day, I immediately looked at Clive. He knew what it meant for me and tried to look pleased but struggled, because he knew that he still had a few months of his sentence to go and he would have to serve out his remaining time without me. Even though I felt sorry for him, nothing could stop the enormous grin that was spreading across my face.

Free, at last.

With Christmas day falling on Saturday that year, the bank holidays meant that the mill was closed until Wednesday. As you might imagine, particularly since losing Mam and Dad, Christmas didn't hold much excitement for me and that year in particular I couldn't wait for it to be over, so that I could start work. The way I looked at it, the sooner I started work, the sooner I would have some money to spend, something I'd never had.

That Christmas was memorable for something – our Madge spent all day every day singing the new hit Christmas song. She wasn't the only one, it seemed that everywhere you went someone was singing Bing Crosby's White Christmas.

Little did any of us realise that 60 years later that song would still be being played to audiences all over the world.

Finally, after the longest few days I can ever remember, Wednesday arrived.

I jumped out of bed at 6:30am, washed in cold water, threw on my new overalls, gulped down my fat and bread and was ready to leave – there was no way that I could wait for the kettle to boil that morning!

I was on my way by 6:45am. A little voice somewhere inside me kept telling me to walk, as I had plenty of time, but I kept ignoring it and threw myself into a series of lung bursting runs, only slowing up when I got to Acre Mill.

It was only 7am when I got there and work didn't start until 7:30am, so I went to talk to old Harry, the maintenance man at the mill. Harry was always there early, so that he could make sure that all the machines were ready for when the weavers arrived. He'd been at the mill for as many years as anyone could remember and must have been at least 60 years old when I started that morning. Everyone either knew Harry, or knew of him and, even after all the years of looking after the machines, he still enjoyed his work and was known for being cheerful and for his pleasant, easy -going nature.

"By, thou art keen to start wark, young Joe, it's only 7 o'clock." Harry greeted me as I walked into the mill.

"Aye, I want to make a good impression."

I didn't think I'd said anything funny, in fact I was deadly serious, but on hearing my reply Harry burst out laughing.

"Wait until you've been here a few weeks." He chortled to me.

I didn't know what he meant and told myself that he must laugh at everything and that's what people meant when they said he was always cheerful.

It wouldn't be long before I understood exactly what Harry had meant.

Ada arrived and took me into the mill weaving shed, where I was introduced to my weaving looms - six in all! Suddenly, the machines started up and the noise was louder than anything I'd ever heard before, it was deafening. The woman that was going to teach me how to run the looms leant over, put her head right next to mine and shouted in my ear.

"Don't worry lad, you'll get used to the noise and learn to lip read."

I didn't get used to the noise, or to the smell of the oil. From that first morning, I didn't like being there, feeling that I was in a cage and longing for the freedom of being out on the moors.

Despite not wanting to be there, I kept telling myself that the money was good and reminding myself how long I'd waited to be able to buy myself some new clothes. So I kept telling myself that I'd get used to it and that it would get better, but it didn't and every day was harder for me to take than the one before.

The Saturday morning after my first pay day saw me head straight to the shops, to kit myself out in some new clothes. It soon became clear to me that, despite my wages being a fortune to me, I was far short of being able to kit myself out from head to toe and that wasn't going to change, no matter how long I stared at the price tickets!

A decision had to be made, should I get myself some new shoes, or a new pair of trousers, or a new shirt? I thought everything through carefully, weighing up in my head the pros and cons that would apply depending on which item of clothes that I bought. Finally, I made my mind up, told the shop assistant what I wanted and made my purchase. When the assistant started to wrap it in paper, I told him not to bother – I'd wear it there and then.

I left the shop and went to meet up with Clive. As he saw me walking towards him, a grin spread across his face.

"By 'eck, Joe, that's a smart looking raincoat." Clive said by way of a greeting.

"I thought tha'd like it." I replied.

"I thought tha' was going to get kitted out wi' everything."

"I couldn't, it all cost more than I thought it would. I'll just have to get one thing every payday."

"So, what made you choose to get the raincoat first?" Clive continued, as he was fully aware of how embarrassed I always was to be walking round in trousers and shirts that other rags would disown if they were able to!

I explained the logic of my choice to Clive - as long as I was wearing the raincoat, people wouldn't be able to see the state of all my other clothes!

In the years since we grew up, Clive often reminded me of that raincoat, recalling how I wore it everywhere, whatever we were doing, such was my shame at how my other clothes looked. I can still see him, laughing his head off as he recalled looking across at me when we were in the pictures, to see the sweat running off me, because I was so hot, but me still refusing to even undo one single button.

As I've already indicated, the skills needed for working in the mill didn't come easily to me. No matter how many times I was shown particular things, when it came to do them again I would often do them wrong.

One particular morning, I replaced the spool in one of the looms. Unfortunately, I'd forgotten to take the used, empty spool out first and, as a result, when the loom was started back up, the spool exploded from it and shot across the mill like a missile.

Luckily, it managed to miss everybody, but that didn't spare me from the ire of my workmates.

Suffice to say, whilst I hadn't got used to the noise, that was the day that I learnt to lip read!

After I'd been there for three months, as I was finishing my work one Friday evening, the mill owner, Mr Frank Bailey, came over to me.

"Now, young Joe, I think we are going to have to give you a week's notice. I know you might be disappointed, but, to be fair lad, I don't think you're cut out for working in the mill."

If he really thought that I would be disappointed then he would have been surprised when I agreed with him, smiled and thanked him for the three months' work.

My time in the mills was over, almost before it had even got started.

38
WHAT PRICE A BIT OF FUN?

After leaving the mill I went working full time as a farm-lad. I loved the work and being on the land and working outside, but the money was not very good. That said, word got round the farmers that I was a good worker, so if a farmer wanted me to go and work for him I asked for more wages and, on most occasions, it worked.

One farm that I liked working at was called Stott Fold, which was owned by Billy and Nancy Moor. They had four young daughters and I think Billy only wanted a farm-lad because there were five females in the house and he wanted some back up!

I got on well with Billy and enjoyed working with him and, to this day, we are still friends.

When I'd left school, Ada had told me to open a bank account and try and save some money, which I did, putting away a little bit of every pay that I earned. Now I had enough money to buy a motorbike! I'd already passed my driving test, on the farm tractor, so now wasted no time in taking and passing my motorbike test. As soon as I'd passed it I withdrew my money from the bank and invested it in a motorbike.

Clive already had his own bike by that time and, once I'd got mine too, we would race around the village like idiots, not realising for a moment the danger we posed to other people and to ourselves. If we rode like idiots at the best of times, I have to admit that we were even worse when we had a lass on the back, when we just had to show off!

Whilst some people just hurried to get off the road when we were approaching and were just grateful to have survived, others were quick to let us know what they thought of our riding 'skills'. To this day I remember one woman in Ickornshaw, Mrs Shaw, who would shout at us as we roared through the village. Her voice was louder than a foghorn and we could hear every word she was calling us above the noise of the motorbikes. Even writing this now I get a shiver up my back and I can hear her voice as clearly as if she was stood outside the door cursing me.

Despite the fact that I loved working on the farms, by the time I was eighteen I wanted to make more money. Clive and me had heard that a firm were looking for lumberjacks to work all over the country and that the pay was good. We decided to go for it, so went together to apply for the job. The interview wasn't very long.

"We want to apply for lumberjack's jobs," I told the firm's boss.

"Have you two done this kind of work before?" The boss man asked us.

"Oh, yes." We both lied.

"You both start next week."

Interview over.

The fact that the only things that we had chopped down were little trees for firewood, or the odd branch for the bonfire, didn't bother us at all. We were convinced that chopping down trees would be easy. If we'd known how big the trees were that we were going to have to fell, we might not have been so quick to lie about our expertise!

I didn't know at the time but taking this job would change my life for ever.

Before we left, we were told that our first job was going to be in Bury St. Edmunds and that it was expected to last a few months. We just nodded as though it was an everyday occurrence for us.

"Where the heck is Bury St. Edmunds?" Clive asked, as soon as we were outside.

Neither of us had travelled very far at all and we didn't have a clue where Bury St. Edmunds was.

"We'll have to look it up on a map." I told him.

"Hell, Joe, it's like going abroad! It's hundreds of miles away!"

Clive's voice echoed my own surprise, when we finally found it on a map.

"Thank God the work's van is picking us up. If we had to ride down on our motor bikes we'd each have a sore arse!" Was all I could come up with by way of reply.

Soon enough our big adventure had begun. The excitement that we felt when we were picked up by the van soon disappeared, as the drive down seemed to go on forever, but, finally, we arrived at our destination and wearily got out of the van and booked into our digs.

The next morning we were picked up bright and early and taken to the estate where we would start our tree felling. We couldn't believe how big the trees were, they were massive and we were still stood, rooted to the spot, looking at them when the foreman came over and gave us each an axe.

There were no chainsaws back then and trees were hand-felled using axes, so anyone experienced at felling would feel right at home with one. Clive and I looked at our axes, looked up at the trees, back at our axes and then at each other. Having walked a few steps away after giving us the axes, the foreman had turned and had watched this little performance.

"You two buggers have never done tree felling before, have you?"

We knew that it was pointless lying, so, sheepishly, admitted that we hadn't.

I was sure that we were going to get sacked before we'd even started, but instead, much to our surprise, the foreman gave us our first lesson in how to fell a tree. Over the coming days he continued to teach us, showing us how to fell the tree safely, so that it fell where you wanted it to fall and so that nobody ended up with a tree coming down on top of them. It was quite a skill to fell a tree, but we soon mastered it and very quickly the foreman was happy enough with our new-found ability to let us work without him having to keep a permanent eye on what we were doing.

Some might say that letting us work without constant supervision after such a short period of instruction was dangerous, but the trees mostly fell roughly where we wanted them to and we didn't kill or maim anybody, so I think the foreman got it right!

Whilst we were in Bury St. Edmunds, each Friday and Saturday night we would go into town to check out the local talent. This one Friday, the foreman said that he and some of the men were going to a club and asked if Clive and me would like to go with them. Neither of us had been to a club before, so we jumped at the chance.

When we got there we didn't know what to expect, but were happy enough to find that it was like a posh pub with dancing. All the pubs we'd ever been in were well lit, but this place was a bit dark. After we'd worked out that the lighting was meant to be shadowy and wasn't just the result of some bulbs having blown, we christened it 'secret lighting'.

Clive went to the bar and got us two bottles of beer. As he handed one to me he told me to make it last, as it had cost him five shillings!

We were standing, slowly drinking our beers, when this woman came up and asked me to dance. She must have been at least twenty five and was fit, so, with a grin to Clive, I went to dance with her. After we'd danced, we chatted a little bit and then I went back to my beer.

Next thing I know, Clive said "Ey up, Joe, that woman's coming over again. I think she fancies you." Feeling quite pleased with myself I got up dancing with her again. Next thing I know, she's running her hand up and down my leg.

"Crikey," I thought, "She does fancy me."

With that, she leant her head forward so that her mouth was resting against my ear.

"Why don't you come back to my place for some fun?" She breathed.

Before I could say anything, she continued,

"It won't cost too much."

I couldn't get off that dance floor and back to my seat quick enough!

"What's up, Joe?" Clive asked.

"It's that woman. Remember what your father told us about mucky women? Well, she's one of 'em!"

If the lighting had been better, Clive would have seen that the colour had drained from my face.

"Nay, never, she looks fit." Clive replied.

"Well you go and ask her to dance!" I spluttered. "She said I could go back to her place and have some fun and she wouldn't charge me much."

"I bet she'd charge you more than five shillings." Clive said with a laugh.

Having got over the shock, we were still talking and laughing about the 'mucky woman' when we got back to our digs. As you might guess, when we innocently told the foreman and the other men about it they nearly split their sides laughing.

What, with mucky women and beer costing 5 shillings, we decided that the club wasn't the place for us.

39
THE MOST IMPORTANT SANDWICH OF MY LIFE

After our experience of the clubs of Bury St. Edmunds, me and Clive led a very quiet life, going to work every day before returning to the safety of our digs. None too quickly the job there came to an end and we were both pleased, not just to be leaving Bury St. Edmunds, but also because we were being kept on. Over the next few months we saw a few places that we'd previously never even heard of. Truth be known, we knew almost as little about the places when we left them as we did when we had arrived, as, still scarred from our Bury St Edmunds' experience, we didn't venture out very often, spending long days at work then returning to our digs where it was early to bed.

One day, as we were nearing the end of the job that we were then doing, the foreman told us that as soon as we'd finished we were heading to a job on a small estate in Cullingworth. He told us that it was only a small job and that we'd only be there for a few days, but we didn't care, we were going back to Yorkshire and we couldn't have been happier.

There was an extra bounce in our step and huge smiles on our faces when we went to work that first morning in Cullingworth. I think our being so cheerful must have got on the foreman's nerves.

"Why are you two so bloody happy?" he asked.

Neither of us answered, but our smiles spoke for both of us.

"You won't be smiling as much when you realise that the nearest place to get something to eat is the transport café a good half mile up the road" he continued.

He was wrong though, as our mood stayed happy as, a little later, we walked to the café to get something to eat.

We were sat there, chatting away about nothing in particular and eating our sandwiches, when the door opened. We looked up to see a young lass and an older man walk in. Each carrying something, they made their way straight through into the kitchen. Clive and I looked at each other.

"That's a fit looking bird" we both said at the same time.

No sooner had we said it than the kitchen door opened and they both came back out, before turning and walking through into the posh part of the café.

I don't think she even noticed that me and Clive were sitting there and she certainly didn't realise that we were both watching her every move as she made her way to the posh part, still accompanied by the older man.

I don't know what it was in particular about that pretty lass with such a wonderful smile that complimented perfectly her golden co-loured hair, wearing a dark grey coat that was fitted at the waist such that it highlighted her slim figure, that made me look at her in a way I'd never looked at a lass before, but the effect she had on me was both immediate and incredible.

"I'm going to marry that lass!"

I made this declaration to Clive as soon as she'd disappeared from our view.

"You've got no bloody chance."

Clive laughed as he said this, perhaps not realising at the time that I was deadly serious.

I wasn't going to be put off by Clive, or anyone else, so I waited until Betty, the daughter of the café owners, was on her own behind the counter. As soon as she was, I got up and went across and asked her who the lass in the grey coat who'd come in with the older fella was.

"Oh, that's Joyce, she's my best friend. She's with her Dad, he's the local butcher who we get our meat from."

"So she comes in here quite often?"

"Oh yes, she's often with her Dad and we get all of our meat from him."

Once again, a broad smile spread across my face.

"Why do you want to know?" Betty asked me.

"Because I want to ask her on a date" I told her.

I was hoping that she'd go and get Joyce for me, but, even as I was about to ask her, Clive appeared by my side.

"Come on, Joe, we should be back at work already and we've got half a mile to walk to get there."

My smile vanished as I turned and, with Clive, headed for the door. Just as we opened the door, Betty called over to me.

"I'll let Joyce know that you're interested."

My smile was firmly back in place as I walked through the door.

By the end of the day, Clive was sick of me telling him what a nice name Joyce was, how I was sure she'd be at the café the next day and how I was certain that I was going to marry her.

The next day I was back in the café. I looked around in the hope that Joyce would be there, but she wasn't.

As soon as she had a minute, Betty came over and told me of the conversation she'd had with Joyce after I'd left the previous day. Apparently, she'd told Joyce that a lad who came into the café wanted a date with her, but Joyce had just laughed and said that a group of them were going dancing in Bradford that weekend, so she wouldn't be free even if this mystery lad asked her.

I was disappointed, but not put off.

I was back in the café on Monday, hoping it wouldn't be too long

215

until Joyce came in, because I was determined to stay there until she did, but knew that if I was too long I'd be in trouble at work.

All of a sudden, the door opened and Joyce and her Dad came in with the meat delivery, taking it straight through to the kitchen.

When they came out of the kitchen, Joyce's Dad started talking to Betty's parents and Joyce walked over to see Betty.

Now was my chance.

I could see Betty pointing me out to Joyce as I got up from the table and walked over to her. I've never been one for fancy talk, so I introduced myself, said that I was working in Cullingworth for a few days and then asked Joyce if she'd go out on a date with me.

I was over the moon when she said that she would.

*

Whilst this book was being written, I asked Joyce what she'd thought about me, that day in the café as I'd gone over and asked her out. She said that she liked the fact that I was tall and had dark hair. She also said that she noticed that I had nice, straight, white teeth, which she said was the clincher, as she could never have gone out with someone who had unsightly teeth.

Our first date was in Keighley and I was at the bus stop waiting to meet Joyce off the bus twenty minutes before her bus was due in.

It was a warm evening, so we spent most of the time just walking around the town, chatting and getting to know a little bit about each other, before going for a coffee in one of the coffee bars in the town centre.

I was on top of the world and didn't want the evening to end, but all too soon the clock seemed to have leapt forward and it was time to say goodnight. I had my motorbike then, so I told Joyce that I'd take her home, but she said her Mam didn't like motorbikes and had told her never to accept a ride on one, so, as slowly as I could, I walked her back to the bus stop.

I didn't feel sad as I watched that bus drive away along the road, because I was so happy – Joyce had agreed to let me take her out again.

Once we'd been out a few times and were well and truly dating, Joyce took me home to meet her Mam and Dad. I don't remember being nervous, but if I was, it didn't last long, as both Joyce's parents put me at my ease straight away. I think that any nerves that I did have were eased by the familiarity that I felt about Joyce's house – firstly the fact that she lived on a farm, but also the fact that the smell of her mother's home baking that filled the kitchen was just as I remembered Pondhill's kitchen smelling when Mam had been alive.

I should point out that the word 'farm' was where any comparison between Joyce's farm and Pondhill started and ended. Although the buildings were old, Joyce's Dad had completely renovated the whole farm so that it was something Pondhill could only ever dream of being – it was modern and the living accommodation was warm and comfortable. Suffice to say, Joyce didn't have to hurry across the dark farmyard when she wanted to visit the closet.

That first time that I met him, Joyce's Dad told me that he hoped I wasn't scared of hard work, because I'd have to work night and day to keep Joyce in the manner that she was used to. I didn't know whether he was serious, or joking, but knew that, even if he was serious, nothing was going to put me off.

Once Joyce and I started courting, I decided it was time for me to change jobs. I was glad to leave tree felling behind for two reasons: firstly, now that I was in love, I didn't want a job that could mean that I was regularly away from home; and secondly, I had never felt comfortable about cutting down magnificent trees that had nothing wrong with them. I sorted myself a new job and arranged to leave the tree felling at the end of that week.

My new job was at a quarry, driving one of the machines. When I'd heard about the job and decided that I wanted it, I went straight to the quarry. They must have seen how keen I was and recognised that I would indeed work as hard as I told them that I would, because they gave me the job even though my age meant that they had to take out special insurance for me to drive the machines - I was only 21 and you normally had to be 25 to drive them.

I worked long hours, but it was one of the top paid jobs in the quarry, so I didn't mind. I'd already decided that one day I wanted to have my own haulage company, so the job proved to be a good platform for me. Not only did I get a lot of mechanical experience, maintaining the machines, but I also learnt a lot about tarmac and stone, getting a good understanding of which types of stones are best suited to the different aspects of road and buildings construction.

40
PLANNING A FUTURE TOGETHER
– BUT GOODBYE TO AN OLD FRIEND

Joyce and I had been courting for about two years and I found myself thinking more and more frequently about asking her to marry me.

One particular day, we had been to see Billy and Nancy Moore at their farm, which was up Cowling Hill. We had a lovely meal with them and were in good spirits when we left. Joyce was wearing a dress and her high heels and, as we were saying goodbye to Billy and Nancy, I remember thinking how beautiful she looked. I decided to tell her, in my own romantic way.

"By, Joyce, you look right pretty in that dress and those high heels, but you'll never be able to walk all the way down Cowling Hill in them. Get on the back of the bike and I'll ride us down t'bus stop. Don't worry, tha' mother'll never know."

We sat in the Dawson's Memorial bus shelter, overlooking Ickornshaw hamlet, having a kiss and a cuddle while we waited for the bus. All of a sudden the time just seemed right, so I broke off from the kiss we were half way through and looked straight into Joyce's eyes.

"I want to marry you. Will you marry me?"

Joyce looked a bit taken aback, but it was only a few seconds until I heard the best word I'd ever heard in my life.

"Yes."

As soon as Joyce said it she burst into tears, which she assured me were tears of joy.

As we sat there in that bus shelter, happily talking about our future together, what neither of us realised was that we were looking down on the house and the shop in which we would start our married life.

The first opportunity that I had, I went to see Joyce's Dad, to ask his permission for me to marry Joyce. I was a little nervous, but not worried, because over the last two years, as he'd got to know me, he'd always been kind and supportive towards me. Joyce had told me that her Dad was impressed that, against the odds, as he saw it, I'd grown into such an honest, hard-working lad, particularly given that as two young kids my sister and I had been left to fend for ourselves.

Anyway, I asked his permission and he shook my hand and gave us his blessing.

We got engaged on Joyce's nineteenth birthday and I couldn't have been happier than when I saw the look on Joyce's face as I slipped a solitaire diamond ring onto her finger.

As soon as we were engaged, we started looking for a house that we could buy and start our married life in. This happy task did though make me face up to something I'd known I had to do, but, because it made me sad to even think about it, had been putting off.

Whilst Joyce and I had been courting, Madge had married Crumack and they'd moved out of Pondhill. Just as I'd feared, theirs wasn't a happy marriage, but, despite Ada and I repeatedly voicing our concerns, Madge had married that man anyway, so there was little more that I could do.

Given the long hours that I was working at the quarry, I had little or no time to spend on the upkeep of Pondhill and it was really starting to show. On top of that, because Joyce and I were saving every penny that we could, I didn't have any spare money to pay for the growing number of repairs that the farm demanded. With every passing month Pondhill was suffering and I feared that it wouldn't be long until its state of disrepair was such that it would once more resemble the neglected shell that it had been when Mam and Dad first bought it.

Pondhill was where I'd lived all of my life and it was where all my memories of Mam, Dad and Meg were based. On top of that I knew how proud Mam and Dad had been, not only to buy Pondhill, but to have renovated it and I knew the amount of their time, blood, sweat and tears that they had invested in making it into what it had become. My heart told me how sad Mam and Dad would be at the decision that I had made, but my head told me that they would have understood why I had made it and would agree that it was the right decision to make.

I went to see Madge and told her that we had no option, we had to sell Pondhill.

Whilst the sale of Pondhill was going through, Joyce and I found the place that was to become our home. A cottage and shop in Ickornshaw were on the market and available immediately. The shop had been closed for over a year, but we quickly decided that they were exactly what we needed, with Joyce, who had worked in retail and had experience of window dressing, excited at the prospect of opening our own shop.

The farm was sold and, as sad as I was to see it go, I knew that my share of the proceeds was going to go a long way towards Joyce and I buying the house and shop in Ickornshaw.

We pressed on with the purchase of the house and shop.

Funnily enough, the house and shop had been owned by the late Mrs Emmot and the shop was the very one where, as a scruffy kid, I'd gone with Clive to spend the pennies given to us by Mr Binns for delivering the slop buckets from the school.

*

Thinking back to those early school days, I don't think anyone, least of all me, would have believed that one day that kid dressed in rags and covered in slop spills would be the owner of the shop where he went to buy a penny's worth of sweets.

We were both so relieved when the purchase finally went through, because we'd fallen in love with the idea of living in the little house, even though it had no bathroom and shared an outside toilet with the people next door.

With endless enthusiasm we set about getting the cottage ready for us to move into and the shop ready to open. We managed to get a grant from the council to install a bathroom and Joyce asked if I'd mind if we had a pink bathroom suite. I told her she could have whatever colour she wanted, I just couldn't believe that we had our own cottage and that, for the first time in my life, I was going to have an indoors toilet.

The shop was Joyce's department and she immediately explained to me why the existing brown paintwork had to go and be replaced with something bright, cheerful and more welcoming. Pink and grey was what she chose and, armed with a paintbrush, set about transforming the place.

We both spent every bit of spare time that we had doing bits to the cottage and the shop. We wanted the cottage to be perfect before we moved in, which meant that everything had to be completed before Saturday 7th October 1961, our wedding day.

41
A Very Happy Man

The day before the wedding I stayed with Clive and his parents at their home. Clive was my best man and did his best to persuade me that we ought to go out and have a few drinks, but all that I wanted to do that night was to go down to the cottage, to check that it was real and I wasn't dreaming. I felt that I was the luckiest person in the world, marrying the girl of my dreams and, at last, having a proper home.

As I lay in bed that night, I thought about how much my life had changed. I thought a lot about Mam and Dad and, despite my sadness that they could not be there the next day, I knew how happy for me they would have been and that they would have been filled with pride. I thought of Pondhill and all of the good and bad things that I had experienced growing up there. I thought about Denis, Ada and Madge, recalling both happy and sad memories and again wishing that I'd been able to do anything that would have made Madge see Crumack the way that I saw him. I thought about Meg, how inseparable we'd been and how much I still missed her. I thought about Clive, Norman, Maurice, Andrew and Peter and the adventures that we had shared as we grew up.

I fell asleep thinking about Joyce, the happiness that she had brought into my life and how I could no longer imagine a life without her by my side.

I woke up with a smile already spread across my face to welcome the best day of my life.

The wedding was taking place at St. Paul's Church in Denholme, the same church where Joyce's Mam and Dad had been married and where Joyce had been baptised. With Joyce being the only daughter, her mum had gone over the top with the wedding plans. I don't think Joyce wanted a big fuss, but her Mam was having none of it, her daughter was having the full works, including the church bells and choir.

The wedding was at 2pm and, from first thing in the morning, I was rushing Clive, constantly reminding him that I didn't want to be late. In the end he gave up telling me that we wouldn't be late and just let me prattle on.

We got to the Church at 1:30pm and were met by the vicar, who took me straight into the vestry and gave me a bill for seventeen shillings and six pence (17/6).

It remains the best 17/6 that I have ever spent.

Clive and I then sat in the front pew, waiting. It seemed like an eternity until I heard the organ start to play and everybody stood up. I stood up and turned to look back up the aisle and there was Joyce, walking towards me on the arm of her Dad. I didn't take my eyes off her until she was stood by my side. I think that in that moment her Dad and I must have been the proudest people in the world.

I'd like to tell you the detail of the wedding ceremony, but, I just spent it gazing into Joyce's eyes, a silly smile planted firmly on my face. As long as I live I will never feel happier than when I heard the vicar say 'I now pronounce you man and wife'.

After the wedding, when we went to our cottage for the first time as man and wife, I was overcome with such a feeling of complete happiness and contentment. As we walked into the front room, we were greeted by the sight of the fire burning in the grate, thoughtfully lit ready for our return by our wonderful neighbours Lily and Leslie, who became dear friends of ours. We both just looked at each other, smiling, no words necessary to voice how happy we both were.

As a wedding present, Joyce's father had agreed to stock the shop for us, a very generous present, which gave us a great start. So it was that we spent our honeymoon going around warehouses and filling the shop. The only downside to the wonderful present from Joyce's parents was that, because he was doing the paying, Joyce's Dad had to accompany us on all of our warehouse trips. I've still never met anyone else whose father in law accompanied them on their honeymoon!

Joyce had decided that at the front of the shop we would sell food, whilst at the back of the shop we would sell clothes. With both parts of the freshly decorated shop well stocked, J and J Sawley opened its doors for the first time.

I soon found out something I previously hadn't known about my wife – she could sell anything to anyone. She would even have been able to sell fridges to the eskimos!

On top of that, Joyce threw herself into community life, organising fashion shows in the village hall, coffee mornings for all the adults and arranging a visit to the shop from Santa for the kids, to name just a few of the things that she did.

Opening the shop meant that we needed to make another investment – in a van, so that Joyce could get to and from the warehouses to keep the shop well stocked. Knowing as many people as I did, as soon as word got out that we were in the market for a van we had a number of people telling us about vehicles that they'd heard were for sale, which they thought would be ideal for what we wanted. They were all trying to help, but Joyce and I had decided that we were going to buy a new van.

We went around a number of garages and car showrooms looking, until we saw this one particular van and, as soon as we saw it, both knew that we would be driving it home. I might have had what some would call an unconventional upbringing, but one thing it had taught me from a young age was to learn from every experience that you have. Without their having realised it at the time, watching my Mam trading her home-made products, my Dad buying and selling animals and Ken bartering to buy his land motor, had taught me the art of bargaining. I put my skills to work and a few minutes later shook hands on the deal that bought us our first proper vehicle.

And what a vehicle it was - an A35 van. To us it was like a Rolls Royce and we couldn't have been more excited if it had been.

Given Joyce's enthusiasm and her selling skills, it was no surprise that the shop was a great success and did very well for us.

I soon realised another of my dreams and started my own haulage firm, which, through a lot of hard work, also did very well for us.

So there you have it. Despite everything, there I was, all grown up, married to the girl of my dreams, living in our own house and running our own businesses.

What happened after that? Well, that's another story.

Suffice to say that, wherever we are and whatever we are doing, no man could be happier than I am when I'm with Joyce.

So if anyone ever asks you what became of Young Joe from Pondhill, all that you need to tell them is that he is a very happy man.

THE END

A Final Word or Two

This book would not be complete without me saying a few words about some of the people who feature within its pages.

Firstly, I'd like to mention my childhood friends: Clive; Norman; Maurice; Peter; and Andrew. Everybody has friends when they are young, but I feel especially blessed to have had those particular lads as my mates. Throughout the traumas of my childhood, losing my Mam, my Dad, and then Meg, my friends were amongst the few constants in my life. As well as true friendship, they offered me support above and beyond that which lads of their age should ever be expected to provide.

I can't speak highly enough about them and whatever words I used to express my feelings about each of them would fall short of describing what I was trying to convey. Suffice to say that I feel privileged to have been friends with each of them and I am both happy and proud that my friendship with each has lasted throughout our lifetimes.

Better friends no man has ever had.

I'm sure that you readers are wondering what became of these wonderful lads, so I'll give you a brief update about them:

*

Clive   My best mate through childhood, from the time that we shared our first day at school, Clive and I remained best friends through all of our adult lives. Clive ran his own haulage business in Yorkshire, before settling in Ross-on-Wye with his partner Pat. Clive passed away in July 2011 and not a day goes by that I don't think about him and miss him;

Norman   Norman married Shirley and, with their daughter

Victoria, they lived in the local area, where Norman ran his own business as a coal merchant. Now a widower and retired, Norman has been a great help in our putting this book together, enthusiastically trawling his memory to confirm facts and details about some of our adventures which feature in this book;

Maurice   Another of us who ran his own haulage business. Married to Pauline, they brought their two sons up in Maurice's childhood home, Court House Farm, where they still live to this day;

Peter   The famous one amongst us. Peter became an actor and has spent a successful career on stage, in films and on television, where he is probably best known for playing Kevin Webster's dad in Coronation Street. Peter has always stayed living locally and was awarded an MBE in 2011 for services to amateur theatre in West Yorkshire;

Andrew   Having spent most of his adult life living in Australia, Andrew has now returned to Yorkshire, to enjoy his retirement.

*

Other than my mates, there are others who featured greatly in my childhood and in this book, who you might wish to hear about:

Ken and Edna   Continued living at the farm until they retired, after which they lived out their years locally;

Ada & John Stayed living locally throughout their marriage. John passed away in the late 1960's, with Ada, never re-marrying, living locally until her passing in 2011;

Ethel & Leonard   Lived out their years in Yorkshire;

Denis   Denis married and, with his family, lived the rest of his years in Yorkshire;

Madge   My sister's marriage to Crumack didn't stand the test of time and ended in divorce. Madge re-married and, with her husband and sons, relocated to Peterborough. Madge sadly died in 1994, aged 58.

Whilst I have the opportunity, I'd also like to thank Mr & Mrs Haggas, the current owners of Pondhill, for their kindness in letting us visit the farm, to reminisce and to take photographs and for themselves providing us with a photograph of Pondhill for inclusion in this book.

Thanks to Curtis Cook for giving his kind permission for us to use his photograph for the book cover, and thanks to Andrea Patterson for taking the stunning photographs of the Yorkshire moors.

Thank you to Martyn Weaver for bringing to life old photos.

A huge thank-you also goes to our publisher Tracey Lewis for all her help, guidance, and patience. Without her the book would not have been published.

As for Joyce and I, well we celebrated our golden wedding anniversary in 2011 and I can honestly say that throughout our time together I could not have been happier.

Joyce and I have done so much with our lives over the years. We've always worked hard, but that was no hardship to us, because that work ethic had been handed down to both of us from our parents.

I must also say that, whilst our life has involved a lot of hard work, it is a world removed from the hard life that my parents had.

We spent our working lives living in Yorkshire and, whilst we've never lived extravagantly, our hard work has allowed us to live comfortably. Certainly, my experience of life as an adult bears no relation to what I considered to be the norm during my childhood.

With animals featuring so much in both of our childhoods, as you might have expected, throughout our marriage we have always kept dogs, having either one or two Labradors at any given time. As well as our dogs, for a time we also owned two horses.

Whilst we no longer live in Yorkshire it remains very close to our hearts and we regularly return 'home' to catch up with all of the wonderful friends that we still have there.

Thank you all,

Joe.

Wedding day 7th October 1961.

50 wonderful years later our Golden wedding anniversary.